RIDING

the

DRAGON

RIDING

the

DRAGON

The Power of
Committed Relationship

RHEA POWERS & GAWAIN BANTLE

North Star Publications
Georgetown, Massachusetts

North Star Publications
P.O. Box 10
Georgetown, MA 01833
(508) 352-9976 • FAX (508) 352-5586

NOTE

*This book and the exercises herein are intended to inform readers and to
expand their self-knowledge. This material is not intended for and should not
be used as a substitute for medical, psychiatric, or psychological counseling
and/or treatment by qualified professionals. The publisher disclaims liability
for any use of this book or its content for other than the specific intentions
designated above.*

Rhea Powers and Gawain Bantle, using the approaches described in this
book, conduct workshops in the U.S., Europe, and other locations. For
information about their schedule and their products, write:
P.O. Box 6546
Santa Fe, NM 87502

Cover design: Arroyo Projects Studio
Cover illustration: Brian Lies
Editor for North Star Publications: John Niendorff

Printed in the United States of America

ACKNOWLEDGMENT

We would like to acknowledge all of our teachers—not only those whose work we have participated in, but also those who have participated in our work. The vulnerability and honesty of the people in our groups has taught us much about ourselves and about the mystery of being human. Because of their trust, we have been able to experience making a contribution.

DEDICATION

To Ruth and Wolfgang Bantle, with love and appreciation.

CONTENTS

FOREWORD

We fell in love and started living together. It seemed simple at the time. We thought we were only together because we were in love. Gradually, we began to discover that our deeper selves had their own intentions in drawing us together. We began to realize that relationship was the perfect way for us to wake up, to discover our own essence.

We have written this book to share our experiences with relationship as a tool for self-discovery. The book is based on discoveries we have made about what seems to work in relationship and what doesn't seem to work. We acknowledge that the parts of our psyches that like certainty and control would love to have a set of instructions, a foolproof guide for living in an intimate love relationship. They'd like to know that certain behavior will produce a predictable result. It would be a comfort to those parts of us to know that if we do *this* and *this*, then *that* and *that* will happen. However, relationship, by its nature, is a more formless process. Rather than yielding a list of specific facts, relationship is an intangible web of connectedness between souls.

The life force expresses itself into Life as an ever-changing kaleidoscope of energies. There are many ways for an individual to begin to explore the kaleidoscope. Living in a committed relationship is one of them. We write about that particular path, as it is one that we, ourselves, are walking. If it is a path you are also walking, or are interested in, we hope our observations will add to the depth and richness of your experience of the journey.

The ideas in this book may be difficult at times. Your emotions or your own unresolved issues may get touched, as some of the material and the concepts may be confronting. At times, your buttons may get pushed. That is to say, you may find yourself having a strong reaction to what you read in these pages. At other times you may discover that you have lived what you are reading. Our approach in this book may challenge the perception of reality you are used to or are comfortable with. That is fine. This is an exploration. We are on an adventure in consciousness and we invite you to join us.

1

THE HERO AND THE DRAGON

Call the world, if you please,
The veil of soulmaking
Then you will find out
The use of the world . . .
                    —John Keats

W hat nourishes your soul? Where is the manna in your life? If the flow of your soul brings you to living in relationship, it is because relationship is part of your path to awakening. We are here to awaken. As Keats suggests, being in the world is about forging our soul—it is about becoming conscious of who and what we are.

Many myths speak about the dragon. The image of this primordial creature still speaks to us from the collective unconscious, as the worldwide success of Steven Spielberg's movie *Jurassic Park* clearly indicates. In Western mythology, a confrontation with the dragon forces the hero to gather all of his resources in order to overcome the beast. In the traditional dragon myth, the hero goes out into the forest, which, in the symbolic language of myth, represents the uncharted territories of the psyche. There, the dragon waits for the hero and challenges his strength, courage, and awareness.

The dragon can be seen as a representation of powerful, primal forces within our own nature that are, for the most part, unconscious. These forces carry with them patterns of manifestation as well as latent resources and strengths that remain unconscious unless we find the courage to confront the dragon and bring the forces it represents into conscious awareness. That is the only way this unconscious material can be integrated into the personal

1

psyche and eventually claimed as a conscious resource that is then contributed to life.

In the myths, the dragon guards a treasure. If the hero is to claim that treasure for his own, he must confront the dragon. Additionally, as Joseph Campbell, the late professor of mythology and author of one of the most comprehensive studies ever written on the place of myth in the evolution of consciousness, points out, the hero's journey is not complete until the hero returns to the community with the prize that was won through the confrontation and, in one way or another, offers the prize for the common good.

An inherent part of the hero's journey is sacrifice. One must leave the comforts of the known and journey out into the unknown. There is a price to be paid, a sacrifice to be made. The confrontation with the dragon is dangerous. The hero can be lost. The hero can be wounded. The hero can die.

In the myths we are rarely confronted with the demise of the hero, however part of the pattern associated with the hero's journey is that in confronting the dragon, in wrestling with those unconscious but powerful parts of his or her own Being, the hero faces the threat of real loss. The journey toward consciousness requires a sacrifice. At the same time, there is the potential of great reward. To repeat, the dragon guards a treasure. The hero, to claim that treasure for his/her own, must be willing to make the necessary sacrifice and do what is required to confront the dragon.

For us, being in a committed relationship is a hero's journey. It is a hero's journey of awakening. The title of this book is a metaphor for the process of relationship as we experience it. Relationship is a wrestling, a struggling with your own inner dragon, that—if done with totality, courage, and awareness—carries within it the possibility of embracing your inner forces and claiming the inner gifts that your partner has helped you to discover. Our observation is that these new qualities contribute to the evolution of consciousness—they help Life in its unending search for new possibilities.

When you view the dragon as holding the potential for self-discovery, the dragon becomes your ally on the hero's journey. This is the shift in awareness that allows you to recognize that the dragon is not an obstacle to be overcome but a friend that can actually take you where you want to go.

It is the awakening of this awareness that allows you to ride the dragon—and enjoy the ride!

For the contemporary hero who is attempting to wrest consciousness from the jaws of the dragon of unconsciousness, the sacrifice—the death—is usually that of a previously held (and hence comfortable) perception of self. It is important to recognize that even a negative perception of self is comfortable, because it is familiar. We cling to our identity for good or ill. Truly, we must die to the old to be born to the new.

In the encounter with the dragon we are changed—we are transformed. Our old structures on the inner and often the outer planes are replaced by a new order. That new order includes part of the old, but is augmented by new, formerly latent parts of the totality of the individual. Then, when the hero returns to the world and shares his/her new consciousness with others, a contribution is made, and the collective consciousness expands.

For the uninitiated, the dragon you wrestle with often looks like the Other, the man or woman with whom you are in relationship. However, as you begin to wake up to your totality, to all of who you really are, you discover that the dragon is, indeed, the otherwise unlived, unclaimed potential of your own soul. The real dragon is that part of your own Being which is waiting to be discovered, confronted, and finally embraced through the encounter with the Other. In this way, if such is appropriate, these previously unconscious aspects of your Self can be consciously brought forward into life as new possibilities for humanity.

As we begin, let's take a little time to lay down some groundwork so we have a common basis for what lies ahead. Most people already have an idea of what a relationship is and what living in a relationship implies. Perhaps it means living with someone, sharing another person's life, having fun with each other. Perhaps it means getting married, maybe having children, and creating a home together. For us, those expressions of relationship are only marginally important. Yes, on the surface these activities are often what the relationship appears to be about. However, it is our perception that the activities around which the relationship seems to focus are not what the relationship is really about. We suggest that the real purpose and opportunity of relationship still lies waiting to be explored.

Through your relationship you can discover who you really are. Ultimately, when you look beyond outer appearances, nobody else is there but you, your Self. (From time to time we may capitalize "Self" to distinguish your essence, your totality, from your personal levels of "self." The personal self is connected to the world of form. It is that part of you that includes your body, your personality, your thoughts, emotions, and psychological patterns, as well as your history, education, and conditioning. The Self is that part of you that is beyond the limits of form—beyond the personal levels—the part of you that is connected to the transpersonal, or transcendent ranges of consciousness. The Self is that part of you that is divine in nature, that is connected to All That Is and thus is connected to Source, or to what people call God.) On a deeper level, the Other is an extension of your Self, and his/her seeming separateness is just Maya, an illusion, a superficial view of reality. The two really are one.

While this may be something you can grasp intellectually, beginning to live your life as if you and the Other are one is quite a different thing. When you open yourself to the possibility that you and the Other are, in fact, in some mysterious, unfathomable way connected and are extensions and reflections of each other's essence, then relationship, life, and the world become a mysterious place of learning and discovery, where whatever is happening to you, whatever is revealing itself to you through life and through your partner is, indeed, manna for your soul in the making.

This book has three main elements. The first, the body of the text, presents our major philosophical perspectives and their implications. These have evolved from our experience in our own relationship and our observations in working with thousands of others on relationship issues in our seminars. The second main element, the "Riding Lessons" section (beginning on page 171), is the nuts-and-bolts part. It offers exercises and meditations intended to give you a direct experience of the material in the book and to deepen the intimacy in your relationship. The third main element—which is interspersed and intermingled throughout all of these pages—consists of references to the transformation of consciousness which is required in moving from viewing a relationship as something *to do*, or as a *thing*, to experiencing a relationship as a living organism whose life is being lived out in a cosmic mystery play, of which we all are both expressions and reflections.

Joseph Campbell wrote that being in a committed relationship is an ordeal. What? I didn't sign up for an ordeal! I thought I was getting a ride into the sunset! It's a nice image, but that's not how things are. A committed relationship is an ordeal in the fullest sense of the term—a discipline, a passage, an initiation into a new level of development. Through our interaction with the Other, we can come to know our Self. If we come to that interaction with awareness, we have the opportunity to wrest a bit of consciousness from the grip of the vast Unconscious and thus support the Divine in manifesting in this world of form.

Most of us would prefer to retain our adolescent images of romantic love, in which the blissful couple does ride off into a happily-ever-after sunset. Wouldn't we? Perhaps that preference is what guides the hand of the housewife from her shopping cart filled with hamburgers and frozen orange juice to the shelf of romance novels conveniently placed by the checkout counter of the supermarket. We prefer not to think about real life, which is what comes after the last page of that book or after the last frame of that romantic movie—where boy finally gets girl, or girl finally gets boy. Instead we sigh, daub at our eyes with rumpled Kleenex, and go home to finish the laundry or pick up after the kids. No one likes to acknowledge that the real work of being in a committed relationship starts after the sunset fades out in the final scene of the movie.

The arduous work of self-discovery through relationship usually begins when one of the partners notices certain aspects of the other partner's personality that had previously gone unnoticed. Often these aspects are ones the observing partner doesn't like so much, or may even be shocked by. If that gap between the imagined, preferred version of the other person and the version which is slowly revealing itself—the not-so-preferred version—is not bridged, the relationship will usually deteriorate in one way or another. The partners may separate, or the respect vanishes, and/or resignation sets in if that gap between the image one held of the partner and the way the partner is actually behaving is not examined and dealt with. It is here, in confronting one's illusions and what one has projected onto the Other, that self-discovery begins. This is difficult work. However, it is not as difficult in the long run as burying the pain of disillusionment or of the loss we feel when our expectations are not met.

If the partners separate, they will either look for a new partner or, if they have played the game of changing partners often enough, they may give way to cynicism and develop a whole philosophy about relationship and marriage based on their disappointments and their unacknowledged pain. If people never question the mechanisms involved in intimate relationships—the mechanisms of the attraction of opposites, of the avoidance of pain, and of projection, the mechanisms involved in attempting to maintain separateness and avoid intimacy—they stay basically blind to the opportunity for self-discovery and awakening that a relationship can present. And that is a loss.

We are writing this book to provide you with a way to identify and deal with those mechanisms, to circumnavigate the obstacles and hindrances that show up in relationships, and to point out some of the joys and possibilities that may otherwise be missed along the way. Our intention is to suggest a context within which to hold your experience of relationship so you can, bit by bit, become a master of the "ordeal" and of the opportunity relationship presents, thereby gaining some mastery over the mystery of being human.

There are few places where one can go for guidance in this arena that are realistic and, at the same time, respect the spiritual nature of human development. We—Gawain and Rhea—live in a committed relationship. With the exception of a total of fifteen days, we have been together all day, every day, for the last eight years and we have moved through many different stages within our relationship. We have also worked with thousands of people in those years, leading trainings and seminars on personal transformation and spiritual awakening in Europe, South America, the United States, and Australia. In addition to our weekend groups, we lead several trainings a year, some of which last up to twenty-eight days, spread out over a six-month period. In each of the trainings we work with from forty to sixty people and we have the opportunity to get to know them very well and to watch their lives and relationships transform. We have had a chance to see what contributes to an alive and rewarding relationship and what does not.

Through our own experience and the intimate sharing with participants in these seminars, we have begun to recognize some of the unconscious patterns and mechanisms that seem to direct the fate of most relationships. We speak from our personal experience with each other, experience gained through painful hours of tears and anger, through blissful hours of laughter and recognition, and through our work with courageous people all over the world who are committed to their own awakening. Drawing on what we have learned in this crucible of experience and on our continuous attempt to confront the seemingly chaotic mystery of life with some degree of consciousness, we will share what has worked for us, so you may have an opportunity to test our observations for yourself and to see what works and what doesn't work for you.

We will speak as if what we say is true, because doing so is easier than constantly repeating "we think" or "our opinion is." Nevertheless, at the same time, we know our viewpoints are not "the" truth. Actually, we do not know if there *is* any such thing as "the" truth. Truth is a dynamic process of change and evolution. The truth at one stage of life might not be the truth for another stage of life. What we are presenting is our truth at this point in our development. This book is not meant as a theoretical exploration but rather as a living experience of the mystery of relationship. What we write is not the reflection of any particular psychological system. Rather, it is what has been developed and confirmed by our own experience. As you read our "truth," we invite you to feel what is also true for you.

We recognize clearly that a committed relationship is not the only path, not the highest path, and certainly not the best path for everyone. It is our path, and if it is also your path, you may find this book useful.

Please note that we tend to speak of an intimate love relationship as being between a man and a woman, because that is the kind of relationship we have. But the mechanisms we discuss are also present in man/man romantic relationships and woman/woman romantic relationships. In fact, much of what we discuss is true in any close relationship and need not have a sexual component as part of the partners' interaction. If you are not involved in a romantic relationship, you will find that many of the dynamics mentioned here will be played out in your relationships with your closest friends or business associates. You can translate what we say to fit your own situation.

2

RELATIONSHIP

When are we ever not related? We are related to what surrounds us. We are related to the air we breathe and, through that air, to all life forms the air sustains. We are related to the world of nature, to the plants and animals which provide the food we need to survive. We are related to the plants that contribute oxygen to the air we breathe. We, collectively, are finally becoming aware that to deny our relationship to our environment may well result in our demise. We are being forced to acknowledge our interrelatedness with our planet and its resources.

Civilization is based on relationship. We buy our bread from the baker who bakes the bread, who received the flour from the merchant who transported the flour, who received the flour from the miller who prepared the flour, who received the grain from the farmer who grew the grain. We are indebted to many, many people who interacted with each other in relationship to produce the loaf of bread we purchase, with which we then nourish our bodies. If we really look at it, we see that relationship is what sustains our life physically as well as emotionally, intellectually, and spiritually. In fact, we can easily say that life *is* relationship. Relationship is what got us here in the first place, through the sexual union of our parents.

Life is the interrelated, interdependent ebb and flow of many forces. These forces are connected through relationship. Relationship is what sustains us while we are in this plane of existence. At death, when we leave this plane, this dimension of interrelatedness, we may find that we move into yet another dimension of interrelated forces.

When we attempt to deny or to avoid relationship, we experience pain. When we try to cut ourselves off from close, personal, intimate relationships (as many do) there is a kind of death—death of an aspect of ourselves that could flower in intimate relationship with another. By denying our connection to one another, we create the pain, the alienation, and the isolation that now appear in so many places on our planet.

The pain resulting from that denial of our relatedness is now clearly confronting the human collective. People are becoming aware that we need cooperation and acknowledgment of our interrelatedness if we are to survive. (The planet itself was here billions of years before we showed up—and it would probably do fine without us.) With the surface of the planet almost totally explored and charted, there are no more wide-open spaces to move into, in which to get away from the rest of civilization and do one's own thing. Doing one's own thing regardless of the consequences to others or to the environment is a luxury we can no longer afford. Only through working together, through relating ever more consciously to each other and to our environment, can we hope to survive. This may be easier to see on a global level than on a personal level. However, the same dynamic applies. If we ignore our personal interrelatedness, if we withdraw our energy from others and attempt to live in isolation because of old pain or fear, we diminish our own life force.

Why do so many people deny themselves the experience of a conscious, intimate relationship? They avoid opening to each other because, in relationship, there is emotional pain. When we open to the vulnerability of love, we also open to the vulnerability of our own pain. We will do almost anything to try to protect ourselves from emotional pain. We will deny ourselves what we want—love, affection, joy, intimacy—in order to avoid emotional pain. There are many reasons why emotional pain is part of a deep relationship and those reasons will be discussed as we go along. For now, let us just note that through the experience of love and intimacy, one's own buried pain will surface.

In early childhood, each of us develops strategies to avoid the discomforts of emotional pain. After that, much of life becomes a tap dance to avoid those situations or those people and events which seemed to cause suffering and pain in the past and which, therefore, we fear might cause pain in the present or in the future. All of the wounds we received in our childhood, the emotional and sometimes physical violence many of us encountered while growing up, leave us with a kind of radar system designed to avoid anything similar in the future. Any time a situation seems to be developing around us

10

which is similar to one we think caused us pain before, we try to avoid that situation and the people with whom it seems connected. In a committed relationship those *Oops, red light! Red light! Warning! Warning!* situations usually don't show up right away, but they do surface after we are already involved and avoiding the perceived danger is harder. These are the difficult moments in relationship. Normally we wouldn't get near "that" experience if we could have avoided it. But here we are with our beloved and "that" experience, the one we would do anything to avoid, is suddenly staring us in the face. Herein, therefore, lies both the gift and the problem with a committed relationship—finally, the only way out is *through*.

When we begin to see that the difficult moments in relationship are actually opportunities to grow, to let go of our defense mechanisms, to get clear, to expand our experience of who we are, then our attitude toward these difficult times changes. While the difficult times are never really welcome, they become challenges and we begin to acquire tools that help us gain some mastery—not only in relationship, but also in life, in the mystery of being Spirit manifested in form.

Often in this book, we will be addressing ourselves to the pain in relationship—to the pain involved in the process of waking up. By "waking up" we mean moving beyond the anesthesia of our conditioning and beyond the illusion of a personal self. For us, waking up means becoming aware of our essential nature as Spirit manifested in form. Clearly, relationship also has many beautiful moments of soaring heights, of connectedness, love, and bliss. These moments are not the problem. When things are going great, no guidance is needed. No counseling and no opinions from others are sought. And so we are concentrating here on those areas in relationship that create problems, that are the products of unawareness and unconsciousness. By focusing on the difficulties with honesty and with as much clarity as possible, one can hope to gain some mastery with regard to being related. Avoiding looking at those difficult moments will never bring any awareness. It will just amplify the problems.

Relationship can be a tool, a wonderful tool, to help one wake up when it is used with awareness. Perhaps it can also support one in reaching that state of consciousness which has been referred to as "enlightenment." Thus, the first element we feel is necessary in order to live relationship as a spiritual path, as a way to wake up, is *commitment* . . . .

3

COMMITMENT

While it is clear that there can be no mastery in relationship if you are not willing to experience pain, it is also clear that you will never allow yourself to experience the emotional pain that inevitably surfaces in a deep relationship unless you are *committed.*

Being committed means that you stay in the process of the relationship no matter what happens. It means you won't run away. You stay and confront what comes up even when it is difficult and/or painful. Unless you are truly committed to the relationship with your partner, your chances of experiencing the bliss, the ecstasy, and the deep enrichment a relationship can bring are severely limited. Relationship as a spiritual discipline, as a way to wake up to the reality of who you truly are, must be a committed relationship. A committed relationship may or may not, however, include legal marriage.

Most religions recognize marriage as a path to God. That is why it is traditionally one of the sacraments or rituals performed in a religious setting by a spokesperson for the particular religion. That is also why the traditional marriage vows, the ones most of us are familiar with, included all of the "for better or worse" possibilities. Those who originally created the vows knew that for marriage to work as a pathway to the divine, one had to stick around.

How do you find the deep commitment that is needed to experience relationship as a path of awakening? There are different ways. In some cases, commitment simply seems to be present from the first time the partners come together. This is grace. This is a gift. Perhaps there is an ancient resonance—the recognition of what seems to be a pre-existing promise between you. In that case, the marriage itself has the feeling of fulfilling a vow from long ago. In other cases, the commitment must be discovered as the partners go along. Sometimes you simply have to jump into being committed to the relationship, even though your outer mind, or rational thought process, might hesitate or want to run away. This latter case may involve more of an intellectual discipline—a commitment to be committed.

If you cannot find within yourself the commitment to go to the end of your path together, you may be better off not stepping into the relationship at all. Stick with casual flings and don't look to relationship as a means of awakening. Find another arena, technique, or discipline that will support you in waking up. And remember, relationship is not everyone's path. If you want to use relationship for awakening, as a way to become aware and to grow, make sure you are with someone who shares that intention. If this is what you want and you are with somebody for whom this is not the case, you are wasting your time. Find someone who shares your intention to be committed.

So, what's the big deal? What does commitment produce? Being committed gives you the space to experience difficult and painful situations without running away, without terminating the relationship in order to avoid the pain. This provides you with the opportunity to move *through* your pain and come out on the other side. If you run away every time your pain begins to surface, you will carry it with you forever. One of our friends once remarked that the only trouble with going on vacation is that you have to take yourself with you. Likewise, if you run away each time your pain begins to surface, you will take that pain into the next relationship. Most people have already tried that at least once. After a while, though, you notice that you are right back where you were in the last relationship, and in the one before that. Only the faces have changed. It gets embarrassing.

Eventually you must swallow your righteous indignation, tuck your pointing finger back in your pocket, and, however humiliating it might be, acknowledge the possibility that maybe—just maybe, mind you—it isn't *them*; it is you. And so, we suggest that it is important to acknowledge your pain as just that: your pain.

Discovering that your pain is yours—that the other person does not cause your pain but merely triggers or reflects it, while you are the one who carries your pain—is the next important element in having a relationship that serves you in your waking-up process. That element is *responsibility*.

14

4

RESPONSIBILITY

Our experience is that no matter how committed you are, sustaining a nourishing and enlightening relationship will be difficult unless you are willing to take responsibility for your own life. The alternative is to play the "victim," and there is no power in a victim stance. You need to be willing to accept that, at some level of your totality, you are the creator of your circumstances. Experiencing the truth of that statement takes time and awareness. If it is not yet your experience, we suggest that you be willing to "act as if" you are the creator of your circumstances. Consider that no matter what happens to you, you are—unconsciously if not consciously—the creator of your life, even if that seems absolutely not to be the case. This perception of reality honors the truth of your divine nature. We do not mean that your everyday mind is the creator of your life or that your personal levels of self call physical reality into being, but rather that some inner dynamic of your psyche is creating your moment-to-moment circumstances exactly the way they are. Even if that is not your experience, just assuming it and using it as a place to come from, as a hypothesis, works.

Perhaps you have noticed that when things didn't go the way you thought you wanted them to go and you felt as if you were the victim of your circumstances, *you* were the person who was always around when *that* happened. (Only the faces changed!) The details in the various pictures might have changed, but the one constant in the various scenes was you. You were there when *that* happened—again! After yet another alcoholic loved one beat you up, after yet another lover stole your money, after another new lover turned out to be married, after one more lover lost his or her job just after moving in with you . . . after you have been through several of those experiences, you start to get suspicious that maybe *you* have something to do with how things turn out (though, interestingly, some people never seem to put that idea together). In this book, however, we assume you have taken this step toward personal responsibility.

Personal responsibility means you acknowledge that some inner dynamic of your psyche, in its wisdom, is causing your life to be exactly the way it is. In its wisdom! It is giving you exactly what you really need. Not necessarily on the level of personal preference, not necessarily on the level of what makes you feel good or look good or what fits some internal or external image you have, but on the level of what you really need. Your soul wants to wake up. The unconscious wants to become conscious. The transpersonal, the Divine, wishes to manifest on Earth—through you.

That's right! Our observation is that you create your circumstances because some part of your psyche wants to wake up. You give yourself the opportunity to confront that which is in the way of your awakening so you can experience it and then move beyond it. Often your pain and your attempts to avoid that pain are what is in the way of your experiencing the fullness of your Being—the joy of being Spirit manifested in form. Therefore, in relationship, if you blame the other person—if you make him or her the source of your experience, or make yourself a victim and want to leave the relationship to avoid those circumstances—you miss the opportunity you created for yourself to grow. Furthermore, you will continue to create the same experiences with other people under seemingly different circumstances. At some point, someone else will trigger your pain and give you another opportunity to experience it and let it go—or you will run away again. Your psyche, which orchestrates your life, will continue to create situations in which your pain is triggered. Your psyche does this in order to give you the opportunity to move through your pain so you can get beyond it. Your psyche is interested in your awakening to the truth of who you are.

All of us identify with our pain. It becomes a part of our internal experience of who we are. Our pain also separates us from others and ultimately from our experience of oneness with Source. This is one reason why a committed relationship, in providing us with an opportunity to become aware of our pain, can be a pathway to awakening. One of our early teachers, Werner Erhard, often said, "What you resist, persists—what you re-create disappears." To re-create is to create newly, to consciously

16

experience something as if for the first time. If you resist your pain (by running away, blaming others, or in any way attempting to avoid it), the pain continues to dominate your experience of life. But if you move *into* the pain and fully experience it, look at it, release the energy and emotion associated with it, and then attempt to move to the original source of the pain (to re-create it), the pain will begin to dissolve. The memory may still be there, but the intensity of the pain associated with the original experience dissipates. As we confront the pain and move through it, the pain loses its hold on us. We begin to experience that we are not our pain. We have pain, yes, but we are more than the pain.

If we have identified with our pain as a part of who we are—"I am the child of an alcoholic," "I was an abandoned child," "I was an abused child," "I am an incest victim"—we can, when we experience and release our pain, know ourselves as more than we have identified ourselves as being. We have all met people who carry their story like an identification badge on their chest. We meet them and we see the badge: "Hello, my name is Tom. My father beat me." We see the body posture, the facial expression, and we wait for the story that is being constantly dramatized and communicated nonverbally. We hear, "Hello, I'm Charlene," and from the body language we know there is a story attached to the introduction. Then it comes: "I was raped when I was six and I hate men." We identify with our pain, with our wound, with our "story," as if it says something about who we are. The more we have identified with our pain, the more threatening is the possibility of letting it go.

Our pain helps to keep the ego in place. The term "ego" is used in many ways by many different people. For the purposes of our discussion, we will define "ego" as that structure within the human psyche that maintains the experience of personal identity. One of the main functions of the ego is to keep us separate from others. That is the ego's job—to provide us with a sense of a separate self. The ego is a useful and necessary tool for existing in the physical world. It allows us to have the experience of being individuals. It orients us in time and space.

The ego also likes to try to run the show. It likes us to think it is the highest authority—that it is in control. The ego gets very nervous when we start awakening to the truth that we are more than a separate package of thought, emotion, cultural conditioning, education, religious background, and social training. In the early stages of the development of our consciousness, we do identify with this package. We think: "This is me—this is who I am." As we begin to awaken to the truth that we are more than that package—that there is an Essence to each human being which is beyond all conditioning, beyond all thoughts and feelings—the ego begins to lose its hold on us. That makes it nervous. That is why it tries so hard to get us to hang on to the status quo.

Surprisingly, the ego does not want us to let go of the pain we have identified with. The ego will do anything it can to get us to drop the whole idea of waking up. And it has a point—waking up is dangerous. Waking up holds the possibility of shattering the entire range of our ego-based self-perception. "Proceed at the risk of losing your image of who you are . . . . "

The process of taking responsibility for the experience of your life is never finished. It expands and deepens as you go along. There is always more you can take responsibility for. By "responsibility," we do not mean burden or blame. Responsibility is not a load you carry. Exactly the opposite is true. The experience of responsibility is a joy, a sudden realization that you are free, that you yourself are the source of your life. Your ego is not the source of your life. Your ideas and thoughts are not the source of your life. Your personal self (with a small "s") is not the source of your life. Your essential Self (capital "S") is the source of your life. That part of who you are which is connected to the transpersonal, to the Divine, is the source of your life and of all life. To feel your connection to Source creates bliss and rapture. To experience it as reality is to move from the immature ranges of your personal psyche into the mature ranges of consciousness that are connected to the transpersonal.

As we move through these pages, we will suggest ways for you to claim more and more areas of your life for which you can consciously choose to be responsible. At this point, however, let us just say that commitment and responsibility are two key elements for having a relationship that will contribute to your awakening.

One of the terms we use in this book is "pattern." By pattern we mean a repeating set of responses or behaviors that consistently occurs in conjunction with particular circumstances. After you have spent a bit of time on this planet, you start to notice that your life is dominated by certain patterns. You notice that in certain situations, you usually react in a predictable way, even when you seemingly don't want to. You notice also that you do, in fact, bring pain and suffering to yourself and to others, even when you don't intend to. When you have lived enough life (assuming a reasonable amount of wakefulness), you begin to arrive at this realization: the outer mind does not shape your life. You recognize that deeper forces are at work, forces that seem to move you into situations and events you would never have consciously chosen with your outer mind. When you arrive at this conclusion, the wish to become aware may arise and you may become a seeker of awareness.

When people start to wake up, they may be attracted to a guru, a teacher, or a charismatic, aware person from whom they hope they can learn to move forward in their own process of awakening. They may become devotees of someone who carries what they seek. People on the path of awakening enter into all kinds of processes. They become involved with ashrams or organizations. They read books, do workshops, and practice various techniques in order to gain the experience of mastery with regard to themselves and to life. Perhaps you have done the same. We, ourselves, have moved through that process. We have spent years studying with all kinds of masters and gurus and teachers and leaders. When we got together and discovered our commitment to our relationship, we also discovered that being in relationship is a true test of how far one has come in the process of awakening.

After having been in many ashrams and spiritual centers and having attended many consciousness-raising groups, we have discovered just how much a committed relationship can serve the process of waking up. For us relationship is its own ashram—its own 'round-the-clock consciousness-raising seminar.

We know that spiritual masters sometimes speak of relationship, particularly sexual relationship or marriage, as a hindrance to the process of waking up. This is not our experience. Our committed relationship has served us in a myriad of ways to become more conscious, more aware, and in this way more blissful and alive. For us, relationship is a way to connect with our divine nature. Relationship gives us the opportunity to recognize ourselves, through the Other, as we really are—to truly know ourselves.

Relationship is an opportunity to come into union with our Self, to embrace and celebrate the totality of our Beingness through the act of embracing and celebrating the totality that is our partner.

In working on ourselves through our relationship, we have discovered some key elements to using relationship as a path of awakening. As we have already mentioned, the first element is the experience of commitment. Another is the experience of responsibility. A third is *understanding the multiple nature of the self*—having the awareness that we, as human beings, are not one entity, but are Beings who contain multiple aspects.

5

MULTIPLICITY

One of the biggest misconceptions we have about ourselves is that we are singular, that the "I" or "me" we refer to in our thoughts about ourselves is a single entity. We think of ourselves and others as if we are just one unit of self. Nothing could be further from the truth. We are not singular. We are multiple. There are many different "I's" or "me's" lurking within us.

Have you ever wondered why you could be serene and loving in one moment and then, in another moment, perhaps only seconds later, be ready to explode with rage or violent anger? Perhaps that rage was even directed at the same person to whom you felt so loving and tender only moments before. Have you ever wondered why, in some moments, you can experience yourself as skillful and centered when confronted with a crisis, yet you feel helpless and out of control in another situation, even if the two situations are similar? Have you ever wondered why a person can be a skillful business leader, able to handle complex problems with ease and clarity, while, at the same time, his or her private life is a shambles?

Most of us are still shocked when we discover that charismatic leaders, be it in politics, religion, or science, have a side to their personality that seems to contradict either their achievements or what they publicly promote.

Have you ever asked yourself: How can I be a certain way (or feel a certain way or think a certain way) and then, moments later, be (or feel or think) just the opposite? Have you noticed that you can have two totally different perceptions of the same situation or person and that each point of view seems totally true for you in the moment you have it, even though the two points of view seem to be in direct opposition?

These things happen because we are not singular entities. We are multiple. We consist of many different inner parts, or aspects. We have an

21

inner community. Some of us have become familiar with the idea that we have an inner child. No! We have an inner kindergarten! We also have adolescent aspects, young adult aspects, mature adult aspects, and, if we are blessed, perhaps a wise elder or two. The personal level of our self has many distinct aspects.

Within our totality we also carry certain animal aspects, with all of the energies and forces associated with those animals. Those animal aspects can be viewed shamanistically as totems or allies, and their energy and characteristics can be used to enhance the experience of our totality.

We also have aspects of our inner community that can open to the transpersonal ranges of consciousness. These are our more mature aspects. There are archetypes within: perhaps the priest or priestess, the healer, the leader, the shaman, and/or the spiritual teacher. There may be angelic and/or demonic aspects available within us now. We may carry inner aspects that connect us to different dimensions—dimensions that have no idea of what life is like as a human in a body.

Each of these inner aspects is complete in itself. Each exists in a world of its own. These different aspects often don't know that other parts of our psyche, other aspects of our totality, even exist. Each of our many inner aspects has its own body language, memories, thought patterns, emotions, and attitudes, and often its own voice vibration. As we shift from one aspect of our inner community to another, our posture may change, our view of life may change, and our voice may shift in timbre and volume. For example, we have all seen an adult receive a reprimand (perhaps from a boss or a partner who has shifted into a disapproving parental aspect) and watched as the adult was transformed into a wounded child—the head goes down, the shoulders come up, and the voice rises half an octave—and the competent adult has been replaced by a stammering six-year-old. Although it looks like the same person is standing there, clearly the aspect which is now dominating that person's psyche is different from the one which dominated his or her psyche only moments before.

At any given moment, one of the aspects of our inner community dominates our experience of life. The reality of that aspect, in that moment, is the reality we experience and express. In another moment, another aspect may surface and then *it* dominates our experience of reality. Meanwhile, having one body creates the illusion that we are only one entity.

22

With most people, different aspects surface as a completely automatic response to external stimuli. Very few of us consciously choose which of our many aspects will dominate our experience at any given time. We are so accustomed to regarding ourselves and others as singular entities that we tend to think in terms of *either/or*. When we have conflicting perceptions of ourselves, or of someone else, we try to make one true and the other false. ("Susan couldn't have embezzled money from her boss; she's such a good mother.") We tend to try to invalidate one perception because another perception exists that seems to be just the opposite of our original perception. ("He always seemed so generous, but here he is being selfish. I must have been wrong about him.")

This applies to internal realities, as well. If you perceive yourself one way and suddenly have a totally different (and sometimes seemingly opposite) perception of yourself, you will most likely tend to think one is true and the other is not. Often, just when you start feeling good about yourself (or your partner), you find yourself (or your partner) doing something really stupid. Most of us have an unfortunate tendency to think: "Ah, yes, that is the real me [or him/her]—the stupid one." We are very quick to put ourselves and others down. Given the choice of thinking of ourselves as brilliant or fucked-up, most of us will opt for fucked-up. Haven't you noticed? In fact, we are probably brilliant in some of our aspects *and* fucked-up in other of our aspects.

As seminar leaders, we were always puzzled that we can be incredibly inspiring, wise, and at times even enlightened in our workshops, and then be petty and vindictive and fight with each other at home. We thought that *either* the parts of us that showed up in the seminars were the "real" ones *or* the ones that got into the fight at home were the "real" ones. We tried to invalidate our professional work because we were not always in the same "space" (or aspect) we were in during the seminars. "How could someone this petty have led that last seminar? I must be a real fake!" (we said to ourselves). And yet, the seminar had been good, we felt satisfied with the work, and we hadn't felt at all as if we were faking.

Next we tried to make the petty one, the one who got in a quarrel, wrong; we thought we should be "enlightened" all the time. We would feel guilty for sitting in front of the television and eating ice cream when we thought we should be reading The Great Religious Texts of the World or be involved in some other activity that was appropriate for someone who worked with people as we had when we were in the seminar. However, once we were introduced by W. Brugh Joy, M.D., to the concept of multiple aspects of self, it all began to make sense. (Brugh was a successful internist who left the practice of medicine after his own spiritual awakening accelerated. He now leads conferences designed to bring the unconscious into consciousness and is the author of the books *Joy's Way* and *Avalanche*.) Finally we could see that, yes, we are this *and* we are that. We have a Teacher aspect that can surface and lead wonderful workshops *and* we have ordinary aspects that can be petty, quarrelsome, and want to do nothing but watch old movies and raise our cholesterol levels.

Perhaps you have felt the desire to get rid of parts of yourself, parts you don't like, parts that are painful, parts that your self-image does not or cannot comfortably include. You may have tried various groups, counseling, therapy, religious practices, and meditation as you attempted to eradicate certain behaviors or emotions from your experience. You may have tried to "get better" or "be different" in one way or another, usually with the hope of avoiding pain.

The desire for change, often motivated by wanting to get away from the experience of pain, is what first brings many of us to the work of personal transformation. This is one of the ways pain can serve us. The desire to relieve pain is often the "carrot at the end of the stick" that guides us onto the path of self-awakening. Our experience in our seminars is that the desire to avoid emotional pain or heal physical illness is frequently what initially motivates individuals to begin working on themselves. However, even though the desire for change may bring us to the path of awakening, we often don't really know what we are getting into. We think we can control what happens. That is to say, we want change in some arenas but not others. And—we want the changes that do occur to be comfortable! Perhaps you will recognize the novice's prayer: "Dear God, I am now ready to step forward on my path to perfect destiny. I am now ready to awaken to truth— as long as no pain, discomfort, or personal humiliation is required." Having been on the path for some time now, we can report that if they're not *required*, pain and discomfort are, at the least, likely. But if people have the courage to confront their pain, the resulting sense of freedom will often lead them into a real desire to wake up and to experience of who they really are. If they do not discover themselves, they may revert to a safer (often intellectual) approach to spiritual awakening, one that is much less demanding—and also much less rewarding.

For those readers who may have been drawn to this book in hopes of "getting better" or "becoming different," we have some good news and some bad news for you. The bad news is that you will never be able to get rid of those parts of yourself you don't like or that cause you pain. The good news is the same: you will never be able to get rid of those aspects of yourself you don't like or that cause you pain. So, you can stop trying to "get better" or "be different." But you *can* begin the awesome, mysterious process of discovering who and what you really are. Your partner can serve you in that process.

Your inner aspects, or selves, are yours forever. The patterns that your aspects carry will never go away. They will never disappear. After years as a rebirther, I—Rhea—have become convinced that your aspects have been yours from the moment you were conceived.

Rebirthing, a process originally developed by Leonard Orr, uses a particular breathing technique to allow a person to re-experience his or her birth. The purpose of rebirthing is to release the trauma held in one's body from birth and to become conscious of one's earliest decisions. Once those early decisions are brought forward, they no longer unconsciously dominate one's experience of life. Often during the breathing, the person moves into memories of being inside the womb.

Over and over again my clients were able to trace a present pattern back to embryonic stages of development. Additionally, after decades of working on myself and counseling others, I have observed that you cannot change your patterns. However, what you can do is to release the pain they carry (usually that of the inner children), so those aspects no longer demand your constant attention. Once you have released the pain of an aspect, it can recede into the background of the psyche (taking its patterns with it) and it no longer needs to dominate your experience of life.

For example, if you carry a rejected child aspect within your totality, that aspect has been there from the beginning. The way that aspect manifests itself in the world is your "story." The "story" (of the rejected child aspect) usually carries pain, which is probably unconscious. Your rejected child aspect may manifest through the story that, as a fetus, you felt that your mother didn't really want a child. Or your story may be that, as a fetus, you felt your parents wanted a child of the opposite sex. A great deal of pain is connected to these feelings. Later in childhood, the rejected child aspect of your totality may manifest through the story that one or both of your parents ignores you in favor of a sibling. Or your mother may commit suicide, or your father might leave the family. These events carry pain which is retained in the rejected child aspect of your inner community.

The manner in which you respond to the story—to the pain that is connected to the feeling of not being wanted—is what constitutes a pattern. You may respond by feeling angry, as feeling anger may be easier than feeling the immense vulnerability of the pain. For example, when I—Rhea—start to get jealous, my immediate response is anger. I find it much easier to get angry and indignant than to feel the vulnerability of the thought, "Oh my God, what if he leaves me?" Or perhaps you respond by withdrawing and attempting to protect yourself from the pain by not feeling anything. Or you may respond to the pain by trying to be what you felt was wanted (by trying not to be a bother, developing the characteristics of a member of the opposite sex, or trying to be like the favored sibling). Later, whenever that rejected child aspect is triggered, so is the response you developed to protect yourself from the unexperienced pain. That response is the pattern you then carry within the rejected child aspect of your psyche.

These patterns are the source of much difficulty later in life, particularly in your relationships. When some event triggers the rejected child aspect, your patterned response also surfaces and you respond in a predictable, or patterned, way. If the pattern includes an angry response, you will get angry. If the pattern is withdrawal, when there is a hint of rejection in your experience, you will withdraw. Most people think what they need to do is change the way they are and not get angry, or not withdraw. However, if you focus on the anger or the withdrawal and try to change your behavior, you miss the gift your unconscious is trying to give you. These aspects and their patterns are being triggered so you can finally feel the pain (not avoid it once again, by whatever strategy) and free yourself of the bonds the pain creates.

Some part of our psyche wants to be free. We want to be liberated from our pain. Some part of our totality wants to let go of the baggage we carry in our personality levels so it can experience the deeper levels of who we are. Therefore, we continue to create circumstances in our lives in which our pain and our unresolved issues are triggered. Thus we continually give ourselves opportunities to release ourselves from the pain that unconsciously dominates our experience of life and ties us to our ego.

If you never allow yourself to feel your buried pain, it gathers energy and unconsciously dominates your experience of life. The more you try to avoid that pain, the more power it has over you and the more it becomes the unconscious motivator of your actions. The more you try to avoid what is inside you, the further you get from your true self. Perhaps, in your effort to avoid feeling the pain in your inner rejected child, you do everything you can in order not to be rejected. You may constantly try to please others so they do not reject you, which takes you further and further away from your own authentic self. You may sell your soul for approval and acceptance—all motivated by the unconscious desire to avoid the (often seemingly devastating) pain stored in the rejected child aspect of your totality.

This basic mechanism applies to pain carried in any of your inner aspects. But the pain is not endless. If you find the courage to experience the pain you carry, it will release you. Once you give those pain-filled aspects the attention they crave, once you release the pent-up energy in those aspects, you can consciously shift your attention to other parts of your Self. You can allow the predominantly child-based aspects to recede into the background of your inner community. They will not disappear, but they can recede. They can stop dominating your experience and your expression of life. Or, you can continue to resist the pain and be unconsciously dominated by the pain you refuse to experience.

You *can* take responsibility for your patterns and embrace the aspects of your inner community that carry those patterns, so you no longer unconsciously dramatize them. You can expand your experience of who and what you are. You can become conscious of who you are beyond the story of your personality levels by releasing the energy that binds you to those levels and then beginning to explore your totality. However, remember that change is not the goal. To become different is not the goal. To be better is not the goal. Expanding your experience of who you are is the goal.

Let's go through that again: though you cannot get rid of any of your aspects, you can let go of the pain contained in an aspect. You can consciously experience the unexperienced pain that is held in any of your aspects and release the energy it contains. This part of the work is based on the fact that *re-creation causes disappearance*, meaning that if you re-create and consciously re-experience an old, unexperienced, and/or repressed emotion, it will cease to unconsciously dominate your experience of life. While you will find that the pain is never totally gone, it will lose its hold over you. It will recede into the background of your psyche.

You may have noticed that even after years of work on the early loss of a loved one or some other traumatic childhood event, you can still dip into the pain of that long-ago experience. However, once the pain associated with the event is consciously experienced, the event will no longer run your life. Its suppressed energy no longer calls automatically, mechanically, for your attention and causes you to play that same old recording yet again.

As we mentioned above, the infantile, child, or adolescent aspects of our psyche usually carry most of our unexperienced pain. And because our psyche does want to wake up, we continue to unconsciously create circumstances that trigger these aspects. We do so in order to give ourselves an opportunity (finally) to experience the pain and let it go. The blocked energy, the unexperienced pain in these wounded aspects, draws us like a magnet when we first begin to go inside. At the same time, we are trying to *avoid* the pain, and this is the source of much internal stress. If the unexperienced pain associated with your mother's suicide is begging for your attention and, at the same time, that pain is terribly threatening and overwhelming to the rejected child aspect of your psyche (which is why it was repressed in the first place), a tension will surface whenever you attempt to explore your inner world. This is one of the reasons so many people never take the time to stop, relax, and look within—it is just too painful. This is also one of the reasons so many people react with the defenses of anger and irritation when their interior is probed, even quite innocently, by someone else. Again, it is too painful. It is also part of why people attempt to go unconscious through drugs, alcohol, food, or other addictive behavior.

As children we did not have the resources to deal with the emotional pain associated with our circumstances. Feeling the pain was too overwhelming for us, so we buried it. However, we are no longer children. Let's look at the calendar and give ourselves a reality check on the present time. We are adults now. We have other aspects of ourselves, of our totality, available to us now, and they *do* have the resources to deal with the pain without being overwhelmed. It is safe to go inside, to release the energy, to feel the pain, and to come out the other side.

Thus, in the process of waking up, one of the first steps we must take is to find those unconscious aspects inside of us that carry the most energy, usually energy in the form of pain. The next step is to release that energy by consciously experiencing the pain, the anger, the grief, and/or whatever else may be there. When we have the courage to do that, we feel lighter, freer, and we have the sense that there is a lot more space inside. Again, however, the aspect that contained the pain remains a part of our inner community and will never leave. Your aspects and the patterns they contain are a part of you just as the color of your skin is a part of you. If you carry an "abandoned child" aspect in your inner community, you can experience and release the pain of being abandoned so that aspect no longer dominates your experience of who you are. But the abandoned child remains a part of your inner community. If you are unaware, your life-energy can gather again in that aspect and suddenly you will once more experience life from the perspective of an abandoned child.

Each of us has had the experience of thinking we have worked on a behavior pattern until it was gone, and then, out of "nowhere," it rears its head once again. We get depressed. We may think we have regressed, that all of our work has got us nowhere. ("I thought I handled *that* years ago. Boy, was I kidding myself.") In fact, however, that is not what is happening. We have simply accessed the aspect of our inner community which holds that behavior pattern. The acknowledgment of this truth is what lies behind the almost ritualistic repetition of the phrase "I am an alcoholic" in Alcoholics Anonymous. If you carry an alcoholic in your inner community it will always be there. Any of you who thought you were over the addiction and that "one little glass of wine with dinner would be fine now" understand that your aspects don't disappear.

Imagine the following: You are like a large house with many rooms. The electricity in your house symbolizes the life force. The different rooms of your house symbolize your different aspects. When you flick the switch in one of the rooms, the light comes on. If you switch on one of the aspects of your inner community, that aspect becomes the dominant experience of the moment. Even if you have not been in that room for years, the electrical wiring is still in place and the moment you flick the switch, the light comes on in that room—again! That house has been the way it is since it was built—your aspects have been with you since you were conceived.

What you can do, however, is to be aware. Don't flick the switch! Don't energize the aspect. If you don't want to deal with what is in the room (again!), don't go in and light it up. Remember, your house is huge; it is not a hut—there are plenty of other rooms to discover.

Most people don't know they are multiple, so they live out their lives in only a few of their aspects. They visit the same rooms over and over again. *Boring!* But once they have realized they are multiple and have let go of the excess energy in those aspects that previously dominated their experience, they are free to discover the other rooms of their house. However, most people never recognize this option. This is one reason we work on ourselves and attempt to become aware of those aspects that dominate our experience of life—it frees us for true self-discovery. The wisdom behind the words inscribed above the doorway of the temple of Apollo at Delphi expands to become: "Know thy*selves*."

The knowledge that we are multiple is a magical key. When we know we are a combination of many different forces, some of them contradictory to each other, we no longer try to fit ourselves into one consistent self-image, one version of who and what we are. Then the journey of self-discovery can really begin. Since most people don't live and operate from the awareness of their multiplicity, they are often at odds with themselves. Chained to a single perception of who and what they are, or think they should be, they strive to fit their multifaceted, vibrant life force into a narrow, culturally conditioned self-image—and they sell their soul in the process.

In relationship, knowing about and operating from the realization that you and your partner are both multiple Beings is a great gift. When you look at your partner and know he or she is a composite of many different aspects and forces, just as you are, you can honor your awareness by not attempting to squeeze that person into one narrow perception of who or what you think he or she should be. And when difficulties come up in the relationship, you can recognize that just one of your many aspects, rather than all of your aspects, is facing these difficulties.

It is freeing when you and your partner understand and operate from the idea that who you are is much more than what you are manifesting at any given moment. You can also realize that when problems or difficulties arise, the inner children or adolescents are usually the ones who have been triggered. The moment you can identify the aspect that has been set off within you and is dominating your experience with your partner, you have made the unconscious mechanism conscious. That means you have ceased to identify with that aspect and have enlarged your experience of who you are. Yes, the aspect that has been triggered is present, but it is not all of who you are. Thus, the moment you identify an aspect, you have distance from it and the opportunity to see if another aspect of your totality might be more appropriate to the moment.

In the "Riding Lessons" exercises (p. 171) you will have the opportunity to identify those child, adolescent, and young adult aspects of your inner community that most influence your experience of your life and your relationship. This will make you alert to and aware of those aspects when they surface. When you are aware of which aspect is currently dominating your psyche, then you have that aspect; it does not have you. It is a part of you, yes—but it no longer dominates your experience of reality.

You are not singular. You are many different, beautiful, and sometimes terrifying energies. In a committed relationship, hiding all of your different aspects is impossible. In a long-term, intimate relationship, presenting only those aspects that are ego-enhancing is impossible. Your fullness is eventually called to the surface. This is one of the many ways in which a committed relationship can serve you in your process of discovering who you are. You are the life force incarnate. You are nature, earth, and cosmos unified into a unique expression of itself.

6

PROJECTION

Wherever we look we discover our own inescapable selves. Wherever we step, a portion of our own unknown self steps before us significantly, mysteriously fashioned and projected. Our destiny, our environment, our enemies, our companions—we have built them all. They stalk out of our depth, essential and self-produced. That is why, to the enlightened person, everything encountered is a manifestation of the initiating priest, a spiritual guide able to bestow the key. The shapes of the initiating power change, but always in accordance with our own need and guilt; they reflect the degree of our spiritual nascence or maturity. And they prefigure the transformations required of us, the tasks we have yet to solve.
—Heinrich Zimmer, *The King and the Corpse*

The next key in using relationship as a tool for waking up is *awareness of the process of projection*. However, before we discuss projection, we need to be clear about what we mean by the conscious mind and the unconscious mind. For the purposes of this book, we will define the conscious and unconscious parts of the psyche as follows: the conscious part of the psyche contains all the things you know—all the things within you and outside of you of which you have awareness. The unconscious part of the psyche is just that—unconscious. That is to say, it contains everything of which you have no present conscious awareness. The unconscious occupies a much larger part of your totality than you might ordinarily assume. The conscious mind, in terms of its size relative to the unconscious mind, could be regarded as the last joint of the little finger of your left hand. The rest of the body could be seen as the unconscious.

The unconscious not only determines most of your actions and decisions, but it also, in fact, determines the events of your life. Regardless of what the conscious mind says—regardless of your good ideas, good intentions, and positive affirmations—the unconscious is in charge. Without attempting to tackle the ancient debate between the concepts of free will and predestination, we observe simply that the choices you make flow from a much deeper part of yourself than the outer, conscious mind.

Projection is the psychological process by which you overlay your outer reality with your inner dynamics. Knowing about projection is absolutely essential if you are to use relationship as a means of becoming conscious. If you are not aware of the process of projection, having a relationship serve you in waking up is difficult.

As a result of projection, what you perceive around you is not necessarily an objective reality independent of you, but rather is a reality shaped by your interior forces. For example, if you find yourself thinking that your partner is really being selfish, your perception is not necessarily the truth. You may actually be the one who is being selfish and, since you don't recognize that quality in yourself, you see it manifested in the Other. Because of the process of projection, how you see the world and those around you is not necessarily how they really are. Rather, what you see and experience around you is your own internal dynamic, projected outward onto your environment, just as a movie is projected onto a screen.

Usually you are projecting parts of yourself (both the so-called positive and the so-called negative parts) which you have not seen, which are unconscious, and for which you have not yet taken responsibility. This is particularly true when you are reactive to what you see outside of yourself. By "reactive," we mean you have an unusual amount of energy attached to the particular perception, or that it has a "charge" for you. The more energy you have on something, the more you can be sure that what has touched you from the outside has something to do with what is happening inside you. As I—Gawain—discuss later in the section on patterns and shadows, I once thought Rhea was very insecure during our seminars, and I criticized her for it. When she hesitated in her response to a question, I thought she didn't trust her answer, which convinced me that I was right. Months later, I discovered the insecurity I perceived as hers was actually mine.

What we are projecting on the world around us is our own unconscious material. For the purposes of this book, we will use the word "shadow" to refer to that part of ourselves we do not see, that part about which we are unconscious. Although that term has been used in other contexts to specify the personal unconscious or repressed portions of the personal self, here we use the word "shadow" to represent both personal and transpersonal material that is not currently conscious to the individual.

People generally act as though they like hearing "good" things about themselves and dislike hearing anything "bad." That is not true for many of us, however. Often we are much more inclined to recognize and expect the "bad" in ourselves than to recognize and expect the "good." Because there is a tendency to equate "shadow" with "negative," we want to emphasize here that our shadow is not necessarily "bad." It is simply that part of our totality of which we are not conscious. Often we fail to see our own "good" qualities and project those qualities onto those around us. Our shadow is not our secrets or those things about ourselves we do not like or try to hide. It is those things we don't even know are there. If we know about something—if it is conscious—it is not shadow material.

When you look around your world and see something that angers you or revolts you, it is because that same thing (or quality or trait) lives unconsciously somewhere within you. It is a reflection of a part of yourself that you have not yet acknowledged or taken responsibility for. If you have a really strong emotional reaction to a child-abuser or a wife-beater or an exhibitionist or homosexuals or a thief or a killer or men in general or women in general, you can bet that the very thing you are reacting against is alive and well in some part of your own psyche. When we get into fights with our partners, becoming angry and finding ourselves making our partners wrong and judging them, some of our own shadow material has been triggered and we are projecting it onto them. In fact, the more righteous we are about how wrong *they* are, the more we are defending against recognizing in ourselves the very things of which we are accusing them.

The quality or trait in our partner that is triggering our anger may show up in us in a different form, but we are judging ourselves nevertheless. We had a very powerful example of this during a recent Relationship Training we led for committed couples in Holland. One evening over dinner, we were talking to a couple in the training. The husband, whom we will call Bodan, is from Ghana and has established a successful life for himself in Munich, where he now lives with his German wife. As we ate, Bodan told us about a shaman who came to his village in Ghana when he was one week old and dying. The shaman saved his life with the help of plants and herbs and marked him with a scar on his left cheek. At his parents' request, the shaman stayed in the village.

As Bodan was growing up, the shaman taught him the art of talking to the local plants and leaves to find cures for sickness and other forms of distress experienced by the villagers. Bodan explained to us that the plants would tell his teacher which of them could cure different illnesses.

Shortly before the shaman died (twenty years earlier, when Bodan was eighteen years old), he told Bodan that he had chosen him to carry on his work. The early scar was the mark of being chosen. All Bodan had to do as a sign of accepting the mantle was to place a traditional white garment on the shaman's grave, whereupon the teaching would be his. At eighteen, however, Bodan had other ideas. But two decades later, over dinner in Holland, he was asking us if we thought he should still do something about accepting what his teacher had tried to pass on to him. The conflict between his enjoyment of his life in Europe and the call of his heritage was clear to us and to his wife.

The next day during a session in the training, Bodan started expressing his irritation at his wife for her practice of talking to a toy stuffed dog whenever she had a decision to make in her daily life. He got very righteous and indignant as he warmed to his story of how a "grown woman" not only talked to this stuffed animal but also experienced getting answers from the dog, and acted on those answers. How ridiculous! As his righteous indignation turned to anger, something clicked for us and we recognized what was happening. His wife's behavior was similar to the technique used by his teacher. The technique of using an external object to gain access to one's own transpersonal awareness is the basis of many forms of "readings," from tea leaves to Tarot cards or the *I Ching*. Since he, himself, had rejected the technique (and the mantle of healer/teacher that went with it) and was not at peace with his choice, he had to make his wife wrong for using a similar technique. The anger directed toward his wife was actually the anger of one of his own internal aspects directed toward another of his inner aspects. He was angry at himself for rejecting the role his teacher had offered him. Once

36

we pointed this out to him, he had the grace to recognize the projection. The next time the training met, not only were the couple in much deeper harmony with each other, but they were also planning their first evening workshop in Munich on traditional African healing techniques. Further, the wife was now willing to take back the wisdom she had projected onto the stuffed dog and claim it as her own.

Recognizing your projections is another way that engaging consciously in relationship can support you in discovering who you are. Understanding that what you see in your partner and are reactive to is what you don't see in yourself (even though it is there) gives you the chance to know yourself more completely. By being aware of the process of projection, you come to see that your judgments about your partner say more about you than they do about your mate.

It is very difficult to begin to "own" one's projections. We really do not want to understand that everything we criticize in others has an equivalency within us. When you first start to integrate this awareness, you may find it painful to acknowledge that everything you hate, everything you loathe and can't stand, everything you have ever judged negatively is, at some level, in some form, a part of your own totality. When you realize that the process of projection is itself an unconscious defense against seeing yourself clearly, you can appreciate how difficult it is to recognize your projections and claim as your own the qualities or traits in others that triggered your reaction. Most of us would rather not acknowledge that we carry within us the very things we judge as wrong in others.

On the other hand, if you can hold the concept that, ultimately, who you are is everything, that you are connected to all creation, then perhaps recognizing that you must also be connected to those expressions of the life force of which you disapprove is not so difficult. If, ultimately, you are one with All There Is, then you can't just be one with the parts you prefer. You are one with all of it.

Let's get back to aspects. You have probably had the experience that your partner can seem absolutely revolting to you in the middle of an upset and then, moments later, when the upset has been cleared, he or she seems completely different. How can this be? Sometimes bringing the apparently conflicting images of a partner together is difficult. Your perception changes as the aspect dominating your own psyche switches. What one aspect of your psyche projects onto the outer screen called "your partner" is different from what a different aspect of your psyche projects onto that same screen. When you shift aspects, your perception also shifts, because what is being projected has shifted. What you see in the other person and what you see in your surroundings is a reflection of the aspect in you that is doing the perceiving. What is around you is a mirror of what is inside you. This is what projection means.

There is wisdom in the observation that whenever you point a finger at someone or something, three fingers of your own hand are pointing back at you. (Try it!) That simple gesture will give you clues to your own interior in a way that few other techniques can.

The moment we take responsibility for our disowned material and move toward integrating the parts of ourselves we previously projected outward onto others and then judged as wrong, our experience of who we are expands. "Yes, I am that, too." When we can say that, our experience of our Being expands, and the way we experience the world around us shifts.

We all acquire a self-image in the process of growing up. Any time your self-image is threatened, your ego has a hard time. Taking back your projections, owning the disowned parts of yourself, can be extremely painful. Recognizing that what you judge in your partner is actually a part of yourself can be shattering to your self-image.

In your self-image, you might regard yourself as a nice person, a peaceful person. But let's say your partner can be violent and you have always judged him or her to be wrong for outbursts of violence. (And no doubt you could get any number of people to agree with you!) Now, you hear about projection. Oops! Could that mean there is actually some violence lurking as shadow material in your very own psyche? *Bingo!* Yes, it could! Since you have always thought of yourself as a peaceful person, suddenly discovering that you may carry unexpressed violence can be a major shock to your image of yourself. (But then, why would you be attracted to someone who carries violence?) In fact, you may want to defend yourself righteously from acknowledging this truth. Here, then, is one saving grace of the recognition that you are a multiple, not a singular Being: you may have peaceful aspects *and* you may also have violent aspects. Both are part of your totality. You are not one *or* the other. You are one *and* the other.

This points to another challenge. When you do not own your shadow material, it will be dramatized by those around you. Usually this role falls to the mate. However, it may fall to the children or someone else in your circle. (You may have noticed that the children of ministers often live out those ranges of expression that are shunned by their parents.)

Once you begin to see how subtle and unconscious the process of projection is, you can begin to appreciate the challenge of reclaiming those parts of yourself you have projected onto others. It is often easier to continue to be the victim of a violent partner and righteously make that partner wrong than it is to acknowledge that, yes, violence also lives within you. Most people have seen teachers or gurus who maintain an image of holiness while their disowned violence, dishonesty, or promiscuity shows up in their followers or is eventually expressed through them. Examples of this range from Bhagwan Shree Rajneesh to Werner Erhard and Jim Bakker.

Last year, when our assistant totaled our car and the one she crashed into, it was very tempting to make her wrong. However, since we knew about projection we also knew that we had some difficult soul-searching to do. Since she was driving our vehicle, we were clear that in addition to whatever was happening for her, she was also dramatizing something for us. Looking at the underlying source of the apparent "accident" was very uncomfortable. We saw that after years of creating and maintaining our work in Europe, we had not taken responsibility for our own destructive energy, which was, through the "accident," surfacing and needing to be honored.

When you begin to take back your projections, your sense of self expands and your awareness of who you are increases. When you begin to take back your projections and acknowledge as present within yourself what you have judged to be wrong in others, you need not necessarily act out those qualities in your own life. Acknowledging that you (for instance) carry violence within yourself, that some aspects of your own psyche can be violent, does not mean you must therefore start manifesting violence in your daily life. Again, this is one of the gifts of the realization that you are multiple. You may have violent aspects within your totality. But you do not have to make that violence within you wrong. Nor do you need to allow your own violent aspects to dominate your psyche inappropriately. At times, allowing those aspects that are capable of violence to dominate your behavior may be absolutely appropriate. If you or those in your care were attacked by a person or a beast, your responding with violence might be appropriate.

As you say "yes" to the parts of yourself to which you have previously said "no," those around you will no longer need to reflect it for you. As you say, "Yes, I can be violent," "Yes, I can be selfish," "Yes, I can be self-absorbed . . . I can be promiscuous . . . I can be nagging . . . I can be controlling," then those around you will no longer have to express your projected shadow for you. You may even find that your circle of friends begins to change as you take back parts of yourself you projected on others. Again, the unconscious wants to be made conscious. If you are unconscious of your own violence (or any other quality or characteristic), it will continue to present itself to you until you acknowledge it—until it becomes conscious.

If we take back our projections, if we own our disowned forces, our world will not have to reflect that material for us. If we can own and be responsible for our violence as individuals, acts of violence will decrease in the world. We will not need to create tyrants on whom to project what we have hidden within ourselves.

We—Gawain and Rhea—spend a great deal of time in Germany and we have watched what happened to the West Germans as the Wall came down. Most of them were born after the war or were children during the last stages of the Third Reich. Suddenly there was no "them" on whom the West Germans could project their shadow. In the last half century, first the Nazis and then later the Communists were the "bad guys." That gave the rest of the Germans a possibility to distance themselves from experiencing themselves as "bad guys." It is the same process the Western World went through with regard to the "evil empire" of the Soviet Union. But now the Wall is down. Germany is one country. There is no "them." The German people have therefore brought the neo-Nazis forward in order to have a screen on which they can see their shadow and have an opportunity to finally confront the unconscious Nazi that lives within them—as it does in all of us.

When you start to work in your relationship with the mirror image called your partner, when you begin to see yourself in the Other, to see your disowned parts in your partner, your world changes. Recognizing that what you saw in the Other is actually something you didn't see in yourself is part of the process of taking back your projections. It means you have recognized that what you reacted against was a mirage, a characteristic within yourself that you projected onto your partner. When you really see that, then there is no longer any need to blame your partner and make her or him wrong. In this moment, your partner changes in front of your eyes. It is miraculous. Suddenly you see your partner as you have never seen him or her before. *Ah-ha!* Now who is *really* over there? These moments are very sobering, because you have given up some sacredly held belief about reality, and you suddenly must acknowledge that you were wrong—which contributes to creating true humility.

The process of taking back projections is a necessary part of waking up to the truth of who you really are. In a committed relationship there are plenty of opportunities for this process to occur. If you can let go of indulging your wish to blame your partner and play the innocent victim and, instead, use him or her to learn about yourself, you are a step farther on your own journey of waking up.

This is not easy work. It is confronting and embarrassing to see that what you have judged negatively is actually a part of you. It is also difficult for many of us to recognize that something we thought was so wonderful in the Other is also a part of ourselves. The so-called positive projections can be equally difficult to take back from the screen of the Other and integrate as a part of self.

In working with one's multiplicity and beginning the process of taking back one's projections, being able to *center* is necessary. If we are to wade through the multiple aspects of our psyche, we need a home base, a solid place within ourselves where we can stand and observe the various characters of our unique inner mystery play without being pushed about by them as they vie for attention.

7

THE HEART CENTER

Developing your ability to "center" gives you a way to return to yourself—to open to your innate harmony and find inner peace. When external chaos or internal emotional upsets strike, you then have a place inside yourself that is untouched by either outer or inner storms. Being able to center allows you to expand beyond the current crisis and to access inner resources that can serve you in the crisis and, at the same time, ensure that you are not absorbed by it.

In relationship, being able to center consciously is particularly important. Then, when your partner is upset or angry, or perhaps is blaming you and/or throwing a temper tantrum, you have the opportunity to respond consciously rather than reactively. But if you both "lose it" and get reactivated, if some of your own unconscious mechanisms get stirred up, then all is lost for the time being and a familiar drama will, once again, run its course. If you can stay centered during the chaotic emotional storms that surface in relationships, they blow over much more quickly. Additionally, when you have developed your ability to center, to return to an inner home base, beginning to live a conscious life is much easier.

A relationship can support you in finding this silent center. It will also test your ability to stay centered! Of course, even if you are not currently in a relationship, the ability to center is an invaluable life-tool. Having a silent center to which you can turn in the midst of life's inner and outer disturbances is very useful. Developing this silent center can be seen as a form of meditation.

You may have noticed that we live in a time of collapsing structures. Throughout human history, as well as in the development of the individual

43

psyche, times of outer chaos frequently appear in order to bring new possibilities for evolution and growth. Many outer structures are collapsing today in politics, the church, the family, economics; national boundaries are shifting. Internal structures are collapsing as well, as we move into an age that makes new and often conflicting demands on the individual. The chaos in the world we live in shows every sign of increasing rather than decreasing. We must be able to locate our own center in this transitional stage of the development of humanity.

An inner, or sacred, center is that part of yourself which does not surrender control to the whims of the various members of your inner community or to whatever is happening around you in the moment. It can sustain a perspective that is not involved in those fluctuations. For some people, staying centered is easy. For others, it is very difficult. However centering may be for you, finding your own sacred center and developing it as a home base is a lifelong discipline, or meditation, that is a prominent part of living a conscious life.

Some spiritual disciplines suggest using the breath or the flame of a candle as centering devices. The Tibetan Buddhists have used intricate mandalas. We suggest using the Heart Center. If you already have a centering technique which works for you, that's fine. Nonetheless, we suggest that you try centering in the heart and seeing if it proves useful.

At this point some discussion of the chakra system may be helpful. Different schools of thought describe the chakra system in different ways. We use a distillation of several approaches to the basic seven-chakra system. It was taught to me—Rhea—by my first spiritual teacher, Emile Canning.

"Chakra" is the Sanskrit word for wheel, and it refers to the energy vortices, or centers, in the human body that can be imaged as spinning wheels of energy. Some individuals can see these energy centers and most of us can be trained to feel them. These centers are usually associated with the physical body, however they also include the nonphysical bodies (energy bodies) around the physical body, which are sometimes simply referred to as "the aura." More specifically, they are often differentiated into the *energy body*, the *astral body*, and the *spiritual body*. These energy fields, along with the physical body, are parts of the overall individual energy system which we call a human being. (Although here we discuss only the basic seven-chakra system, we note that there are additional energy centers, such as those on the soles of the feet and the palms of the hands, that are not included in this basic system.)

These seven basic chakras, or energy vortices, run up the midline of the physical body. A subtle energy called "kundalini"—the Sanskrit word for the life force—spirals through the chakra system, running from the base of the spine (the first, or "root" chakra) to just above the top of the head (the seventh, or crown chakra). The amount of kundalini energy that moves through the chakra system depends on how much has been awakened in the individual and how much is still dormant.

Each energy center, or chakra, in the body has specific attributes or characteristics associated with it. These characteristics are actually attempts to label or describe the forces associated with the particular center. We have found that focusing on the Heart Center deepens our capacity to bring the forces associated with the Heart Center into our daily life.

The first or "lower" three chakras (the term indicates relative position and is not intended to imply a judgment of value) are associated with our physical needs and desires—our human self. The upper three chakras are associated with our spiritual self. The Heart Center, the fourth chakra, is the central point in the chakra system. It is the energy vortex that connects our physical and spiritual selves.

The first chakra, located at the midpoint between the genitals and the anus at the base of the spine, is associated with basic survival and primary emotions. The hara or second chakra, located about the width of three fingers below the navel, is associated with sexuality and sensuality—the survival of the species or race through biological procreation. The third chakra, located at the solar plexus, is associated with personal will, personal power, and personal emotions. The fourth chakra, the Heart Center, is located in the center of the breastbone about two-thirds of the way down the breastbone from the throat. (We will focus on the forces associated with this energy center a little later.) The fifth chakra is located at the base of the throat and is associated with communication, creativity, and the expression of the Self. The sixth energy center, or chakra, is located in the center of the forehead, just above the eyebrows. It is also known as the Third Eye, and is associated with inner vision, inner knowing, and inner wisdom. The seventh, or crown chakra, is located just above the top of the head. This energy center is associated with nirvana, the transcendent, enlightenment.

45

Briefly, the forces associated with the Heart Center and their related attributes or characteristics are (we will go into these attributes in greater depth in the Heart Meditation portion of "Riding Lessons"): (1) *Compassion*—the ability to feel with another without losing your own sense of identity; (2) *Innate Harmony*—the ability to center, to locate your sense of self as a stillpoint of consciousness, regardless of what is happening around or within you; (3) *The Healing Presence*—and the ability to channel or transmit that healing energy; and (4) *Unconditional Love*—love that is beyond personal preference or personal judgment, love that does not need to be earned or deserved, love that simply "is." (We must remember that the words used to conceptualize those forces *are* just words, labels that refer to the forces themselves.) As we focus on the Heart Center, these qualities become more available to us.

Staying centered in a relationship does not mean avoiding situations. It means avoiding being dominated by an aspect of our psyche that may be automatically reactivated by the situation and is inappropriate to the current time. The ability to center gives us the opportunity to choose how we will respond to a situation (to choose which aspect of our psyche is going to run the show), instead of operating on automatic. Usually, those aspects that are automatically reactivated by any difficult situation are our very young aspects. They do not have the resources to deal with an adult situation in a way that is appropriate. When we develop the ability to center, we give ourselves the option to choose which aspect of our psyche is going to be in charge of our experience at any given moment.

After we have established the discipline and skill required to center, centering can take place in a couple of seconds—and that brief pause to do so breaks the mechanical nature of most responses to life. This gives us the chance to live consciously, which very few people do. Most people live a reactive life, one that is mechanical, predictable, and at the mercy of the internal and external "weather."

We like to use the analogy of a jukebox. Remember the old-fashioned jukebox? You drop your coins in, make a selection, push the corresponding buttons, and the little arm swings up into the air. The arm hovers over the stack of records, then swoops down and grabs the one you've selected, lifts it up, lays it on the turntable, and the music plays. If you push the button labeled "B-1," then you know exactly which record the jukebox will play. It is predictable. It is mechanical. If you push another button (reactivate another aspect) you will get another record—consistently, automatically. It's a programmed response. Developing your ability to center gives you a moment of choice in which you can choose which record your own jukebox is going to play. But a word of warning: once that little swinging arm has latched onto a record, it's too late. You have to listen to that music yet again. The moment of choice comes just *before* an aspect gets activated. Once the record is playing, changing tunes is very difficult. But then, you've probably noticed that.

In talking about multiplicity, we mentioned that all of us have both personal and transpersonal aspects. A relationship is blessed when you can consciously connect on both personal *and* transpersonal levels—that is, when you like and enjoy each other when you are in your personalities and you can also tune in to the transpersonal levels together. However, one thing that clearly doesn't work is when one partner attempts to avoid a personal moment by moving into a detached overview. When that happens, no real communication is possible. There is nothing more deadly to an alive personal moment in a relationship than an "enlightened" or philosophical response to a partner who has just expressed his or her feelings. ("What? You're annoyed that I invited my family to visit for three weeks without discussing it with you first? You're probably just projecting some unresolved anger toward your own family." "You say you're jealous that I spent so much time with the blond at the party? You know we are really all one in consciousness, so there is no need to feel jealous.") If either you or your partner attempts a distant approach to the situation when a personal response is appropriate, you can bet the "instant guru" is just trying to avoid the discomfort of the moment.

Being centered doesn't mean avoidance, deadness, or a mechanical recitation of some philosophical statement. Being centered means staying present and conscious during what may be a difficult situation. It can provide you with the possibility of being able to shift between various personal aspects and genuine transpersonal aspects. Being centered means resisting the pull of those parts of your inner community that are inappropriate to the current situation (even though they may be close to being triggered or

47

reactivated), and at the same time not trying to escape the intensity of the moment. Whew! Now there's a challenge!

We have talked about some keys to our understanding of how to work with yourself and your partner in order to be more conscious. How do you apply these concepts to real life? If you are already in a relationship and your partner is willing, you are probably ready to start. That brings us to *communication.*

8

COMMUNICATION

Without true communication there is no chance of having a relationship that will be fulfilling and will serve you in your quest to find out who you really are. Many people, however, never really communicate. They just talk toward the other person, and the only thing they really do is listen to themselves. Instead of giving attention to whoever is talking, they are formulating what they are going to say next—as soon as the other person stops hogging the airwaves! Or perhaps they are mentally running through next week's "to do" list. Or they may be so caught in one of their younger aspects or parental aspects that they can't really hear what the other person is saying.

When you are full of yourself or your own internal process, really listening to what someone else is saying is very difficult. So the most important ingredient in true communication is the ability to listen, to hear what your partner has to say. Particularly when there is an upset or a quarrel in a relationship, the ability to really hear each other always holds the potential of producing a breakthrough.

Really hearing your partner, truly comprehending what he or she is communicating, means you walk in the other's moccasins—you are able to know how it is for that person. Often in an upset or a quarrel, you are so busy talking about how you are feeling or how you see the situation that you lose your ability to hear what is happening for the other person. You are so busy trying to be understood that you forget your partner wants the same understanding from you. Once you are into the upset, you may not even care what is happening with your partner, or how he or she perceives the issue. And yet, if you could hear the Other, if you could experience his or her reality for a few moments, there might be no upset. Conversely, when you feel you have been heard, that the other person "got" what you said, an immediate release of tension occurs, and what was an upset or a potential problem often dissolves.

Being able to listen means being able to set aside your own reality for a moment and experience the reality of the other person. The idea of really hearing your partner's communication is based on the same re-creation mechanism we spoke of in regard to pain: what you resist, persists—whereas re-creation causes disappearance. If you resist your partner's communication, it will persist. If something is bothering your partner and your partner cannot tell you about it, he or she will likely continue to carry it around. There is a good chance that he or she will not be able to let the thoughts go, and will be stuck with them. If the thoughts happen to be negative thoughts about you, you would be wise to give your partner the opportunity to let them go by communicating them (even though listening may be difficult).

It is important to understand that this doesn't mean you have to agree with your partner. However, if you are able to experience his or her reality in that moment, if you are able to completely understand and absorb your partner's communication, to re-create your partner's experience, then the thoughts or the opinion or the experience in question will shift. This is a gift we can give to each other. It just makes things easier. If you do not re-create your partner's experience, your partner must find another way to deal with whatever he or she wanted to communicate. The chances are that if your partner cannot communicate and be heard, the thoughts will become solidified. They become more real.

In the "Riding Lessons" section (p. 171), you will find a communication exercise to support you in practicing the major relationship art of receiving each other's communication. We suggest that you practice it several times, following the formal directions. No doubt you will quickly find a suitable informal structure of your own. However, establishing a few ground rules in the beginning is useful, because people are generally not trained in the art of re-creating another's experience. A conscious effort is required to move against the pull of old habits of interaction.

We all know there are times when we just want to be heard. There are times when we just want someone else to know how we feel, to know how it is for us. The same is true for our partners. At such times they may not want to know our reactions or how we feel about what they are saying; they just want us to know how it is for them. Furthermore, because we now know about multiplicity, we can be aware that only one aspect of our partner is speaking. Knowing that what is being said does not necessarily represent our partner's totality makes receiving a difficult communication easier. This is incredibly liberating for both partners. Listening to your partner say something that may, for instance, be uncomfortable for some of your own younger aspects is much easier if you realize that what is being expressed is but one voice among many that reside within your mate.

In addition to the error of thinking we are singular, we also make the mistake of thinking our thoughts are real. We all carry fears of being condemned for our thoughts or feelings. Our own inner judge condemns us. We are afraid to express our truth in the moment because we are afraid of being put in a box, labeled in some way or another, and being eternally "that," without the possibility of redemption. It is so liberating just to say whatever there is to say in the moment, without the fear that the other will blame us or judge us or use what we say against us. Often we know that a thought is not "real," that it is a passing expression of one part of our totality, but we are afraid to express it because the listener may take it as "real" or make it "real" by giving it too much importance. You've had that experience, haven't you? Then you don't express what is there and it keeps floating around in your head, when you know that if you could just say it, you could let it go. Hasn't that happened to you?

At the same time, we are accustomed to making the thoughts of others "real." We usually hear what someone else says as if we were hearing the expression of their totality rather than the fleeting experience of one aspect of their multiplicity. We are accustomed to believing thoughts, whether the thoughts belong to ourselves or to others. This is part of why we resist hearing other people's negative opinions about us and seek out their positive opinions—we think their thoughts say something "real" about us. Or, if we are caught in one of our "bad boy" or "bad girl" aspects, we get others to confirm our thoughts about ourselves by manipulating them into making negative comments about us. We fail to recognize that these negative comments are actually our own unconscious thoughts about ourselves that we have made "real." We operate as if what someone (including ourselves) thinks about us actually says something about who we are. It doesn't.

Remember the discussion about projection? Our aspects project themselves onto an outer screen: the other person. When we remember this, our not making "real" what someone says about us is much easier. This applies to the ego-enhancing statements as well as to the less flattering things that we ourselves and others say about us. Remembering that thoughts are just thoughts (and then only the products of a particular aspect) also helps to keep us from giving our own thoughts about someone else too much validity.

Communication is so important in an intimate relationship that we will run through the basics once again in an effort to encourage you to move through any discomfort that might arise for you and communicate with your partner. So, from the top: once we become aware of some of our own aspects, there may be times when we need to say something (knowing it is only one of our aspects speaking) just to let go of what we are thinking and/or to support us in letting go of that particular aspect. Understanding that our partner has many different aspects and that the aspect we are listening to at any given moment is just that one aspect, one of many our partner carries, makes it easier to receive the communication. Really being heard allows our partner to let go of the thought and creates space for his or her inner experience to transform. The more we hang on to our thoughts, the more real they become. They gather energy and become things of substance that we then need to defend and make right by creating evidence to support them. Then we can say: "See, I knew that . . . . "

If our thoughts gather enough energy, they may eventually come into manifestation. We forget that a thought is originally just a thought, a thing without substance; and furthermore, it is only the thought of one of our aspects. However, if we keep giving a thought energy in the form of attention, it will take on substance. This is part of the power of communication: if you communicate your negative thoughts honestly, the energy connected to them is released and those thoughts are less likely to manifest as reality.

Let's look at an example of what we are talking about. Let's say you have the thought, "My partner is going to leave me." This is typical of an "abandoned child" aspect of the psyche. (Mommy and/or Daddy left, so the abandoned child aspect thinks everyone will leave.) Probably some fear accompanies the thought. You try to put the thought out of your mind, but it keeps coming up. You don't tell your partner about it because you don't want to give him or her any ideas about leaving you. The thought persists. Soon you are looking for evidence that your partner is going to leave you. Naturally you find the evidence you are looking for. Because you are looking through the filter of "I am going to be left," almost anything your partner does or doesn't do can become evidence that the thought is accurate.

The more you hold on to the thought, the more evidence you find that the thought is true. The more evidence you find to "verify" the thought, the more you believe the thought. It creates a snowball effect that gathers mass as it rolls though your consciousness. You become so obsessed with your thought, trying to make it right, being afraid it *is* right, trying to make the thought wrong by doing everything you can think of to make your partner not leave you, that you stop being the person you were. You stop being natural and authentic, and eventually your partner does leave you. Then you are *right*. "See! I knew it! He/she left me." Finally!

The mind loves to be right. What is worse, some of us go through life making such ideas "right" in relationship after relationship. We never see that we are only reinforcing one aspect of our totality—in this case, the abandoned child aspect.

What really happened? We grabbed on to the thought and made it real. We did not communicate it to our partner and therefore let it go. We held on to it. We didn't give our partner the chance to re-create it for us so it could disappear. Instead, we inwardly resisted the idea. ("Oh, no. He/she can't leave me. What would I do if that happened? I mustn't even think about it." But, of course, we do think about it.) When the thought and the fear came up, we did not center and look to see which aspect of our totality was in charge of our consciousness at the time. In fact, the abandoned child became more and more dominant as the thought gathered mass. Finally, the thought gathered enough mass to manifest. Then the abandoned child was "right" and the rest of our totality and the relationship were sacrificed to the domination of the abandoned child.

On the journey of awakening, one of the most important tools to develop is the ability to move beyond the illusions of the mind. We need to develop the capacity to distinguish between the phantoms of the mind and the "voice of God"—between the thoughts of our personal aspects and the inspiration and insight of the transpersonal. To repeat, being able to receive our partner's communication and being able to really be heard by our partner is a great support on the path. Being able to let go of the thoughts from our personal aspects helps release the energy that holds us to the personal ranges of consciousness and it opens the possibility of moving into the transpersonal ranges of our totality. Really hearing each other is a gift. It is a gift we can consciously give to our partner. When we are able to move our thoughts out of the way, we can cease being dominated by our personal levels of self and give God a chance.

The communication exercise in "Riding Lessons" is a good place to start. For instance, we will often stop each other during the course of the day and say, "Can you 'get' something for me?" The other person stops and gives his or her full attention to the moment. (Sometimes the response is, "Okay, in ten minutes; just let me finish this first.") Then the one who wants to be heard starts by saying: "I have the thought that . . . you didn't want to make love this morning because you don't find me attractive anymore." Or: "I have the thought that . . . when your family visits we won't have any time together." Or: "I have the thought that . . . I really don't want to go on vacation next week." Or: "I have the thought that . . . you're getting fat." Or: "I have the thought that . . . I might die of cancer."

The other partner just hears what is being communicated; usually the thought disappears and the day goes on. Admittedly, we've had a bit of practice, and though we rarely get reactivated by such an interchange, it wasn't so easy in the beginning. Using the phrase "I have the thought that . . . " helps. Doing so reminds you and your partner that you know what you are saying is not necessarily the truth, the whole truth, and nothing but the truth. It is simply a thought. What's difficult is when one partner forgets that the thought isn't real and delivers the communication not as something he or she wants to let go of, but as if "the truth" were being communicated. Then having your own material reactivated, rather than your simply being able to receive the communication, may occur more easily.

If, like most couples, you are not together during the day, it would be useful to take time for a short communication session in the evening to let go of anything that came up while you were apart. You might even jot things down as they arise for you ("He left his coffee cup in the bathroom—again!" "She got the steering wheel sticky—again!") so you can get clear with each other when you are together and not let the uncommunicated "stuff" get in the way of being together. It is much better to take a few moments to say "I got frustrated when I found your coffee cup in the bathroom" or "I got my hands sticky on the steering wheel" than it is to suppress the irritation over and over until you explode and create an upset that could have been avoided. If you are away from each other for the night, a phone call at the end of the day is useful. You can keep each other current on what you are thinking and feeling. This keeps you connected and helps to keep the space between you open. In fact, clearing your communication before going to sleep at night is good relationship hygiene, whether you are doing so by telephone or you are sitting together in the same room.

As we grow up—depending on what our cultural, family, and social conditions are—we learn what is all right to talk about and what isn't. We learn what is safe to share and what is taboo. In Gawain's family (and perhaps in yours), talking about sex in any kind of a personal way was difficult. Later, as an adult, he noticed how hard it was to be honest with Rhea in regard to sexuality. In Rhea's family, money was a taboo subject, so she has to be particularly aware not to stop herself from communicating about money.

We all have subjects about which speaking openly is difficult. We are hesitant to reveal ourselves in what we have considered to be a taboo area. These taboos are often unconscious. What arena or subject is most difficult for you to discuss freely? Perhaps it is emotions or feelings. Perhaps it is expressing your admiration or acknowledgment. Perhaps it is expressing yourself about something you want. After a few decades of being careful about what you talk about and how you talk about certain things, you can imagine that your spontaneity and aliveness are limited. So, it is a great gift to be able to be heard, to be able to be listened to, and at the same time to know there is an understanding in both of you that what you are sharing is not all of what you are.

Sometimes it is helpful to be able to feel the emotion under your partner's words. Sometimes you need to be able to experience your partner's anger or sadness or disgust. Centering in the heart is very useful in those moments. Just focus on the Heart Center and breathe. This can allow you to open to true compassion for your partner, no matter what is being communicated.

As with any acquired skill, real communication takes practice. You can't expect to be able to do it by just reading these pages and intellectually understanding them. You learn by being exposed to the fire in the crucible of your relationship. You will fail many, many times. But if you stick with it, you will slowly experience a shift in your communication with your partner.

Bob Larzalere, M.D., author of *The Harmony of Love*, once pointed out that the source of conflicts in any relationship can be traced to one or both of two fundamental experiences. The statements that summarize these experiences are: "You don't get how much I love you" and/or "I love you more than you love me." This insight is an exceptionally useful tool for handling communication difficulties in relationship. If you look under the surface any time you feel hurt in relationship, you will, if you look deep enough, find one or both of these two experiences. After you have peeled off the details of the upset through communicating with each other, what is left when you reach the source of the conflict is, "I love you more than you love me" and/or "You don't get how much I you love you." For example (though this may require a bit more vulnerability than most of us are ready for without some practice): "I'm angry that you invited your family for the holidays without discussing it with me first. I wanted to spend that time alone with you. I feel like it is more important for me to have time alone with you than it is for you to have time alone with me. I feel like I love you more than you love me."

When you recognize that one of these two experiences is running the show, a lot of tension lifts. Instead of losing yourself in the blaming game, which is a defense against your own pain, you can short-circuit the drama usually associated with attempting to defend yourself and come right to the point by asking yourself which of these two experiences is active at the moment. Of course, there are still details to deal with, but recognizing the underlying theme of the upset gives you a new perspective on those details. It also moves you from aggression to vulnerability. Upsets and conflicts that may appear to have nothing to do with these experiences—perhaps a fight about household money or about the education of the children or about the visit to Uncle Harry—will eventually boil down to one or both of them.

Acknowledging this can create vulnerability and be embarrassing, but if you look, you will usually discover that is what's really going on. Check it out the next time a conflict arises.

Another important aspect in the area of communication is the process called "perpetration/withhold." This term was used by the *est* organization years ago to describe a mechanism that shows up in personal relationships and that, in its extended version, is essentially the basis of karma. (The idea of karma is associated with the belief in reincarnation found in Hinduism and Buddhism. It is popularly understood to mean that, in this life, one reaps the benefits of good actions and the punishments for bad actions performed in previous lifetimes.)

Perpetration/withhold *is* a mechanism—meaning that it happens without awareness, automatically. The basic elements are: you do something to someone that you judge as damaging. Then you don't take responsibility for it; you don't acknowledge it and clean it up. Because of your innate integrity, you must then have the other person do something damaging to *you* in order to unconsciously balance the score. If we don't become aware of this mechanism at that point, we then blame the other person for "what he/she did to us" and feel justified for our earlier action. This is the way we "do unto ourselves" what we have "done to others." We unconsciously set up reality so the one we have damaged damages us. Then some part of us can be "right" for originally having done something that our innate integrity judges as having been damaging to the other person or to his or her aliveness—after all, look what that person did to me. We—Rhea and Gawain—have seen this mechanism in ourselves and others so often that we feel it is a brilliant piece of awareness to put in anyone's relationship toolbox, therefore we include it. We also tell you about it because it is one of the strongest arguments we know of for full communication.

Okay. Let's take a look at it. To repeat, a "perpetration" is anything you do to others that you feel in any way threatens their survival or damages their aliveness. It not only may include direct physical harm, but also harm to their experience of life, their joy, their well-being—anything that would hurt them physically, emotionally, psychologically, or spiritually. That covers a lot of territory. Now, we all do such things, either consciously or unconsciously, at one time or another. If we "clean it up" as soon as we are aware of the real or perceived damage, it is fine. That is, if we take responsibility for what we did, the cycle is completed and the mechanism doesn't come into play.

So, if you do something that is in some way damaging to your partner (Thomas says: "Where are the rest of the cookies?" Susan says: "I don't know." However, she does know. She finished them and is too embarrassed to admit she did it—again!) and then you take responsibility for what you did (Susan says: "You know, Honey, what I said just now was a lie. I know where the rest of the cookies are. I ate them.") your partner may have a reaction ("Again?") but the cycle soon ends. However, if you do something that your integrity judges as damaging to the other and you do not "clean it up," if you withhold the acknowledgment that you did what you did (Susan doesn't acknowledge the lie), you *must* have your partner do something to you so you can make him/her wrong and therefore justify your original perpetration.

Two things about this mechanism are important to recognize. First, the mechanism is unconscious. Second, our innate integrity is what decides whether what we do is damaging to another or not. Our innate integrity is not conditioned by society or religion and it is unique to us. Our head, our mind, will try to convince us that what we've done doesn't matter, that it won't hurt anything, and it's not that important—along with assorted other justifications (after all, other people do it all the time) and rationalizations whose aim is to get us off the hook, to allow us to avoid the uncomfortable experience of taking responsibility for our actions. However, what our head says doesn't matter. What other people say doesn't matter. That other people may think nothing of doing whatever we did doesn't matter. If our personal integrity says what we did was not okay, we will make ourselves pay if we don't clean it up. The mechanism is usually so subtle that we don't notice it. We get righteous when we get a traffic ticket (and must give money to the government) but we don't recognize that it happened after we cheated on our taxes (and withheld money from the government).

In relationship, the perpetration/withhold mechanism is deadly. How big or how small the issue is does not matter. It also does not matter if there is actual damage—if you feel damage was done, that is enough to call the mechanism into play. If you do something to your partner which your personal integrity, in any way, declares is damaging to your partner, and you don't clear it with him or her, you have to set your partner up to damage you. Not only does this pay you back (balance the scale) but it also allows you to justify your original perpetration.

The classic example of this, which all of us have seen in others if not lived ourselves, is the following: the husband has an affair. He never tells his wife. The affair ends. Time passes. The wife has an affair. The husband finds out. He is outraged. How could she have done this to him? He leaves her and righteously tells anyone who will listen how terrible his wife was to cheat on him.

Sound familiar? Given the perpetration/withhold mechanism, he *had to* have her have an affair. That allows him to make her wrong and justifies his having had an affair in the first place. At some level, he set it up. (We know two wives, each of whom "happened" to have an affair with the painter her husband hired to paint the inside of the house while he was away on business and his wife was home alone every day. In both cases, the painters were hunks—hired by the later-outraged husbands.)

In the case of the missing cookies, if Susan hadn't come clean about having eaten them, she would most likely have set up a situation in which Thomas would lie to her—or he would accidentally eat the cake she baked for her women's group. Then she could make Thomas wrong. It is a mechanism. When we are unconscious, it plays itself out in our daily life. One way or another, we pay.

The same mechanism applies in terms of a past-life context with regard to the creation of karma. Most people can, with some guidance, experience memories that seem to be from other lifetimes. I—Rhea—was a past-life therapist for several years with a large practice in Manhattan and I took thousands of people into the experience of past lives. If people I was working with went into a "victim" scenario in a past-life experience, I knew there were earlier lives in which they had done the same thing to others that they now experience being done to them. All of my research demonstrates that the need for the pay-back, the creation of karma, only happens when one does not consciously take responsibility for one's actions. The same is true of "instant karma"—those things that happen in the moment-by-moment relationships in our daily lives.

In addition to the karmic pay-back you set up if you don't take responsibility for the perceived or actual damage you do to your partner, any withholding at all in a relationship limits your self-expression. You cannot have a spontaneous, alive relationship if you are protecting something. If there is something you must guard, something you must hide, then you can never really let go. You can never really relax and be completely spontaneous, because if you do, "that" might slip out. Therefore, you must always hold some of yourself back from your partner. You must be careful. How, then, can you ever be really intimate? Obviously, you cannot have the kind of relationship that serves you in waking up if you are not willing to share everything with your partner. You can't have a relationship that is truly free and fun if you are protecting some part of yourself from your partner. That brings us to *secrets and honesty.*

9

SECRETS AND HONESTY

Having a relationship dedicated to the awakening process of both individuals is difficult when secrets or lies are present. In any deep relationship, there must be a willingness to embrace the more difficult aspects of ourselves and our partner. That means we don't hide the truth just because it is uncomfortable. We need to be committed to telling the truth no matter what. This takes great courage. Often men who are physically very strong get weak knees when confronted with the possibility of experiencing the emotional vulnerability of sharing their secrets and/or telling a truth they have been withholding. The courage to tell the truth in our relationships, no matter what the consequences, can be a part of our commitment to the relationship and to our own awakening.

When we grew up, our parents educated us in their philosophy about telling the truth, which usually was: don't lie—except sometimes. White lies were okay . . . as long as we weren't telling them to our parents. It is interesting, isn't it, that we say "white" lie, as if the qualifier "white" diminishes the fact that it is a lie. There is no hierarchy with regard to a lie. Some lies are not better than other lies. A lie is a lie is a lie. Having a relationship that works is impossible if there are lies between the partners, no matter how insignificant they might be.

For most of us, telling the truth takes discipline. Often, lies have become so much a part of our social behavior that we no longer even recognize them. We lie to ourselves as easily as we lie to others. In a committed relationship, however, what works is sharing honestly, however uncomfortable it might be. Doing so also supports you in telling the truth to yourself.

Designating a lie as "white" generally means you don't tell the truth because you think someone might be hurt, or your telling the truth might be uncomfortable, or you think the situation might not be important enough to need the truth. But those little "unimportant" lies will erode your relationship if you don't eliminate them or clean them up once they have occurred. Often a justification for the white lie is that we want to spare someone else from emotional pain. Usually that, in itself, is a lie. In most cases, we simply want to spare *ourselves* from an uncomfortable situation.

For many of us, lying is part of our social training. How often have you refused an invitation on some pretext—"Dinner on Thursday? I'd love to, but I just have too much to do in the office this week"—because it was just too difficult to report the truth: "Actually, I'd rather not have dinner Thursday or any other day, because I really don't think we have very much in common and I don't want to spend that much time with you." Even if such "truths" are withheld out of kindness, being conscious that you are nevertheless lying is useful.

One of the most deadening habits in which many people engage throughout their lives is saying "yes" when the truth is "no," or "no" when the truth is "yes." In our seminars, we continually encounter people who have sold out their truth for so long in order to be socially acceptable, in order to get along, that they no longer even know what they really want. If, just in order to get along, you say "yes" to your partner when the truth is "no," a great deal of resentment will build up in you toward your partner. At the same time, if you say "no" when the truth is "yes" just to protect yourself from being vulnerable, eventually you will also build up a great deal of resentment—toward yourself.

Many times, with children, you will need to tell the truth in a way that is appropriate to their stage of development, but you *can* almost always tell the truth. During one of our trainings in Switzerland, a mother—let us call her "Petra"—discovered that the basis of her inability to connect intimately with her daughter was her own guilt.

During a particular seminar process, Petra suddenly remembered that one time, as a single mother, in a very difficult situation when her daughter was quite young, she consciously did something that endangered the child's welfare. At the time, in a state of overwhelm, she actually had the thought that she wished the child would die. As she had that thought, Petra left the two-year-old girl alone for a few moments on a staircase where there was no railing and the child could have fallen. In fact, she did fall. The child was hospitalized after the "accident," though she had not been seriously harmed.

Petra convinced herself and her family that it had, indeed, been an accident. But some part of her remembered her silent wish to be relieved of the burden of providing for her child, and she felt guilty. She carried this guilt for a decade. Although that memory had been suppressed, in our Mandorla Mystery Training, the memory surfaced and the guilt was uncovered. (We took the name "Mandorla" from the almond-shaped form created when two circles begin to overlap.) Petra saw that she was unconsciously pushing away her child's love because it touched her own guilt. Her withheld communication, her secret, was a filter through which she experienced every interaction with her daughter. If she had fully opened to her love for the daughter, she would also have had to open to the pain of her guilt for endangering the child she loved.

Petra needed to clear the incident with her daughter. For her to go home and tell her now twelve-year-old daughter that she once wanted her dead would not have been appropriate. However, she *could* tell her there was a time when she did not take as good of care of her as she now wishes she had, and that she feels bad about it. (A twelve-year-old can hear that without experiencing any psychological stress.) Petra went home and told her daughter exactly that. When she did, it allowed her to take responsibility for her action. By communicating her guilt, she permitted herself to open fully to the love between herself and her daughter.

The next time the group met, there were a lot of tears among all of us as Petra shared the story of her conversation with her daughter. We were the witnesses as she found her own self-acceptance. The other parents in the group could relate. Petra's courage allowed us to confront that part of ourselves which can (and does) wish harm to another—even to our own children. As a result of Petra's brave struggle toward self-acceptance, all of us in the group were forced to include that destructive aspect of the psyche in our own self-image.

Again, our observation is that any kind of lying in a committed relationship is definitely deadly, and we recommend that the truth be told. We recommend that you also communicate thoughts you consider harmful, since they gather energy and may actually manifest if they are withheld. Like lies, they take up space that otherwise could be transformed into the experience of love and bliss. In the end, at some level of consciousness, everybody always knows the truth anyway, even if the truth seems to be hidden. We are all connected on a deep level and a lie has a certain energy to it, an energy we all notice either consciously or unconsciously. So since everybody already knows everything at some level, no one needs to be protected from the truth. Acknowledging the truth about yourself in relationship with your partner—a lifelong discipline—clears the space for a deepening intimacy.

When we—Rhea and Gawain—started living together in February 1987, we took hours and hours to share honestly all of our history, our dreams, our desires, and what we liked and didn't like about ourselves. We told each other about our greed and anger, we shared our sexual fantasies and secrets, we revealed our little run-ins with the law. We shared and acknowledged all the embarrassing facts about ourselves. Since that time we have essentially been together every day, around the clock. We continue to share things as they come up. We tell each other everything—especially the things we do not want to say, since we know those are the very things that carry a "charge" and will eventually get in the way of intimacy and spontaneity.

We tell each other when we are attracted to someone else. We share our sexual fantasies (which can often lead to delightful results). We tell each other if we have a damaging thought about the other or about the relationship. ("Sometimes I think I'm smarter than you are and I should really be with someone who is at my same level." "I can't imagine I'm never going to go to bed with anyone else for the rest of my life." "When so-and-so hugged me, I got turned on." "I made you wrong to my friend." "I don't want to make love because I just masturbated.") Communicating in this way is difficult and often embarrassing, but it keeps the relationship clear, alive, and spontaneous.

Hiding anything requires energy which is then no longer available for the relationship. When you speak your truth, you don't hold your energy back; you experience yourself as flowing and in harmony with yourself. Further, you and your partner are now aware that "your truth" is, in fact, usually only the momentary experience of one of your aspects and not necessarily the expression of your totality. When you give an aspect attention and let it have its say, it is then more willing to recede into the background of your inner community and allow you to shift aspects, so another, perhaps more appropriate aspect can have center stage. When you withhold or lie, you are so identifying yourself with the action or the thought you are protecting that you think it is who you are. However, you are many, many different selves, or aspects . . . and you are none of them. Who you ultimately are is everything and, simultaneously, nothing—no thing.

When you hold on to a lie, or *any* thought, or *any* action, you severely limit yourself. In effect, you are saying, "This is who I am and I have to protect myself." When you lie, you separate yourself from who you are and limit yourself to what you are protecting. You also will become less and less spontaneous and intimate in your relationship.

We do not recommend telling the truth and sharing your secrets with your partner because it is morally right or ethically superior. We recommend it because it works. If your intention is to create a relationship that is open, spontaneous, blissful, and alive, then telling the truth and sharing your secrets will support that intention. Nevertheless, we acknowledge that the shadow side of this recommendation is *control*. To ask that your partner reveal everything can, from another point of view, be seen as a way of controlling your partner. While we recognize that point of view, our concern here is opening the doorway to full and open communication with a partner. We find that this in itself is transformative in relationship. Most people have never fully communicated with anyone. Most people do not fully acknowledge their truth, even to themselves. Revealing oneself fully to one's partner in this way requires extreme vulnerability, and this vulnerability is precisely what leads to healing and transformation.

10

DISCOVERING AND WORKING WITH YOUR ASPECTS

As we start to become aware of our multiplicity, knowing we have both masculine and feminine aspects within us, regardless of our external gender, is very important. Further, as we go deeper into ourselves, we begin to recognize that our outer partner is an expression of our own internal, countergender aspects. A beautiful passage from Marion Woodman's book *The Pregnant Virgin* points to the dance between the outer and the inner masculine and feminine. She writes: "When the masculine is unbound, and the feminine is unveiled, then together they interact within and without. The penetrating power of conscious masculinity releases the eternal feminine. The woman awakens the man to his own receptive power. He penetrates her; she receives him. He awakens her to her own penetrating power; she awakens him to the presence of his own feminine soul. Together they are put in touch with their own inner wisdom."

Associating the masculine aspects of the psyche with the functions of the brain's left hemisphere may help us to understand the part the masculine aspects play and how they balance with the feminine aspects of the psyche, whose functions correspond with those of the right hemisphere of the brain. Our masculine aspects give us the ability to reason, to create logical structures of thought, to catalog, to discern, to deduce, to distinguish, and to bring into form. Our masculine aspects create in realms which include those of science, theology, commerce, economics, and philosophy. In all of us, the masculine aspect of the psyche wants to be able to see things clearly, to define a strategy and stick with it. It loves clarity and precise analysis and control. It has the ability to abstract, to see things devoid of their emotional content, and to make decisions based on so-called solid facts. The masculine aspects of the psyche are very uncomfortable with chaos and the loss of control. They do not want to rely on anything that can't be known with the five senses or with the precision of the intellect. The masculine aspects of our psyche can't stand not to be able to see clearly or not to know.

In the continuing evolution of the collective psyche, the viewpoints of the masculine aspects of consciousness have been in the forefront for at least three thousand years. That is to say, the values and perspectives of the masculine have guided the development of the human collective, as order and control have dominated religious, economic, and social life. Masculine values, including the illumined mind; abstract, intellectual thought; mind over matter (note that the root of "matter" in Latin is the same as that of "mother"); and the control of nature (both external nature and our internal, sensuous "nature") have been the goal of major religions around the globe. And while religion sought to control humanity's internal nature, science sought to control external nature.

The attempt of the masculine aspect of the collective psyche was to control and thus dominate forces that are ultimately beyond human control and human understanding. As a collective, we attempted to say what behavior and which beliefs were acceptable in order to have some sense of control. Naturally, we also needed to control our neighbors' behavior and beliefs in order to provide ourselves with a sense of our own "rightness" and therefore give ourselves some security in the face of the immense forces of nature.

That which we could not control or understand ("understanding" being, after all, an attempt to control), we denounced. And that which we could not allow in ourselves (because it was too overwhelming to those parts of the psyche that sought control), we could certainly not allow in those around us. The forces of the chaotic feminine within our own psyche, which we could not control and which no laws could contain, were projected onto an outer screen. One such screen was offered by the aspect of the feminine labeled "witch."

The masculine has always projected its shadow onto the feminine. This is apparent not only in Christianity but also in Judaism, Buddhism, and other forms of Oriental religion. In his book *Oriental Mythology*, Joseph Campbell describes a legend of the Buddha written by Ashvaghosha, c. 100 A.D., which has Prince Gautama, the future Buddha, saying: "Such is the nature of women: impure and monstrous in the world of living beings!" Jainism, a religion still popular in India today, extols an almost complete suppression of the body (the feminine) and its desires in favor of a totally ascetic life (the masculine), stating that the highest levels of spirituality cannot be attained by a woman.

Of course, women have also projected their disowned masculine aspects onto the men around them. The abusive or suppressive, dominating aspects of the inner masculine have been projected onto father, brother, and husband and not recognized as part of the women's own interior forces. Women have used the masculine (within their own psyches and projected outward onto the screen of convenient male figures) to suppress their own feminine. Having done so, women could feel comfortably victimized by the men around them, and complain. (Perhaps one or two woman readers might recognize that dynamic in themselves.)

When we become aware that we project the disowned countergender aspects of our internal community onto the countergender people around us, we gain a deeper insight into the collective "battle of the sexes." We can also see that the way we interact with the opposite sex is a clue to the way our internal masculine and feminine interact. Outer reality is a reflection of the inner dynamics of the psyche. That is true at both the individual and collective levels.

We should acknowledge that women as well as men have denounced their neighbors as "witches." That is, both women and men have attempted to control the vast forces of the chaotic feminine by distancing themselves from those forces, projecting them on others, and then denouncing them. As much as feminists would like to cite witch hunts as another display of the suppression of women by men, we must bear witness to the fact that the masculine aspects within women also fear, and therefore move to suppress, the chaotic feminine wherever they find it.

A broader view of witch hunts would acknowledge the evolutionary process of the collective psyche as it moves toward its own maturity and encourage us not to confine our thinking to the level of victimizer against victim. The witch hunts must have been part of a necessary stage in our collective development, since they are what Life called forth. In fact,

Wolfgang Giegerich, in his essay "Advent of the Guest," indicates that the withdrawal of the projected shadow of Christianity from the distant Moslems, as manifested in the Crusades, to the projection of that same shadow (the perceived threat to the belief structure of the majority) onto the women of one's own town, was actually a step forward in the psychological development of the collective. In this shift from the distant East to one's own community, the collective brought the disowned material closer to home, thus opening the hope that eventually we will, indeed, come to recognize the "enemy" as ourselves.

We suggest that regardless of one's preferences and judgments, there is a wisdom to the evolution of consciousness that life manifests. We suggest, as we will later explain in the section on wounds and how they serve, that everything is and always has been perfect—both for the individual and for humanity as a whole. Which is to say that while the way life is may not suit our preferences, there is a deeper wisdom at work that serves our soul. We can "learn from history," not as such learning is traditionally understood (as a caution against repeating the "mistakes" of our forefathers), but rather by coming to see history as a description of the evolution of the consciousness of the collective. "Ah-ha! *Such* are the ways of humanity." "*Thus* it evolves and develops."

As Brugh Joy suggests in his book *Avalanche*, one can learn about the nature of life by observing what it is—not by imposing one's (very limited) judgments of what it should be, or should have been. We suggest that what has been is exactly what was needed to get us to this moment in the evolution of the collective psyche.

It is appropriate, however, to point out that for the past three millennia and then some, people have been in the grip of a masculine approach to the mystery of life. We have been attempting to structure reality through one "approved" set of beliefs after another about the nature of that reality and thus provide ourselves with some semblance of psychological security. Threats to the existing structure were dealt with in a masculine way—get rid of it, eliminate the threat. A feminine approach might have aimed at inclusion rather than exclusion.

We suggest that a shift is now taking place in the development of the collective psyche. The pendulum has swung very far in the direction of the development of masculine values. The stage is now set for an infusion of values and perceptions of those aspects of the collective psyche that are more feminine in nature—of those aspects that are more inclusive, that tend more toward relationship and harmony.

The feminine qualities in all of us (i.e., in men *and* in women) are being brought forward at this time. Some of the qualities of the feminine aspects in both men and women are: receptivity, artistic creativity, the ability to be at home in chaos, and the ability to connect deeply with nature and to surrender to its forces instead of attempting to conquer and control them.

A woman's "moon time" and her ability to feel new life growing inside her and to give it birth bring her naturally closer to the rhythms of life. The ability to nourish, sustain, and heal is innately feminine. Men are discovering the value of these qualities in themselves as they support their wives in giving birth and take over more direct care of the children. Men are consciously beginning to open to their emotions and to explore their ability to relate.

The nourishing mother is one face of the feminine. But the feminine can also destroy. The "devouring mother" is another, though less popular face of the feminine. This is the aspect of the feminine that wants to re-absorb that to which it has given birth. As the full range of the feminine comes forward, we are being presented with ample evidence that its darker aspects are making themselves known. If we look at the escalating number of natural catastrophes on the planet—earthquakes, hurricanes, erupting volcanoes, and floods—we could reasonably assume that Mother Nature is pissed. The forces associated with the Dark Mother—Kali, the Hindu goddess of destruction—are coming forward, as the feminine presents Herself in the collective psyche.

Again, when we talk about the feminine we are not talking about outer gender. Masculine and feminine characteristics exist in varying degrees of development in both sexes. Both men and women carry male and female aspects of consciousness within their inner communities. In some heterosexual relationships, the man carries most of the feminine energy and the woman most of the masculine energy. You have met couples where the woman is the efficient one who holds everything together, while the man is the dreamer, the poet, the artist, and perhaps the one who chooses to stay home with the children as the woman supports the family. That we live in a time when such options are available—when a father may be given custody

71

of the children because he is acknowledged as the more nurturing parent—is an indication of the recognition that traditional role partitions do not reflect who does what best.

In our culture, at this time in the evolution of humanity, both genders are experiencing a great deal of confusion about their roles. Family structures are collapsing and, as we indicated above, society no longer offers a clear definition of the role of a man or of a woman. This is an exciting time, bringing us new possibilities to define ourselves in accordance with our own inner nature rather than with an external model. It is also a chaotic time, as the structures of the past are collapsing in the face of the reality of the present. The chaotic feminine is manifesting in the collective consciousness. The eruption of chaotic forces, both in nature and in the affairs of humanity, is a clear sign that the emphasis on the masculine aspects of the collective psyche cannot continue. The feminine qualities of life, which are inherent in all of us, want to be honored and lived as well. As you explore your inner community you may discover that you also have emphasized the masculine aspects of your totality at the expense of your feminine aspects.

A woman who has only developed her feminine aspects seems more likely to partner with a man who has only developed his masculine aspects. A woman who has developed her masculine aspects and neglected her feminine aspects is likely to choose a partner who has a strongly developed feminine. Individuals who have developed both their masculine and feminine aspects more equally are likely to partner with those who have also developed both sides of the masculine/feminine spectrum. Ultimately, our external relationship with a partner is a reflection of the inner relationship between our own masculine and feminine aspects.

In order to work with your aspects, with the different personalities in your own inner community, you first must begin to be able to recognize at least some of them. Once you are aware of some of them, being able to shift from one aspect to another, more appropriate aspect in both your relationship and in other situations in your life will be much easier. However, if you don't know your aspects, you are basically at the mercy of the mechanical way they get reactivated and you have almost no chance of discovering the recurring patterns in your relationships.

Seeing yourself with any objectivity is very difficult. You may well be the last to know when you are stuck in a particular aspect of your totality. You think the way you're being is simply "who you are." You think it is your "personality." You so identify with the aspects that routinely dominate your psyche that you think they are all there is to who you are. But they're not. (The Aspect Processes in "Riding Lessons" can make you conscious of those parts of your totality that unconsciously dominate your experience and expression of life.)

When you begin to work with yourself in this arena, starting with your child aspects is best. Our workshops have given us the opportunity to observe and interact with thousands of people from different countries and many walks of life, and what we observe is that the inner children dominate the psyche of most of them. Additionally, these child aspects are usually the ones that hold the most unexperienced energy. Remember also that, as we said earlier, your different aspects are rarely aware of one another. The life of each of your various aspects has its own reality. If you have a "rejected child" aspect dominating your consciousness, for example, it may not have done a reality check since 1956. It does not realize that times have changed. When that rejected child is reactivated in you, you are back in 1956. This aspect, the rejected child, has no conscious knowledge of life after 1956. It also does not know that you have other aspects, with other resources, available to you.

The first time you really understand this, you will probably be shocked, for although your conscious awareness relates itself to time, time has no significance for the deeper levels of the psyche. For instance, you may have had an experience of the outside-of-time-ness of the deep psyche in your dreams. Perhaps you have had a dream that takes place as a "sequel" to a dream you had years before. Or perhaps you have had a strong intuitional flash (or a reading from a psychic) that something would happen "soon," only to have the predicted event happen years later. This apparent time delay happens because the deeper parts of you are outside of time.

When the patterning in the rejected child aspect of your inner community was first activated, time stopped. When this aspect initially came forward and looked around, its reality was that it was rejected. It is, by definition, not in touch with current reality. Thus when that patterning is again activated and that aspect dominates your current experience of reality, you too are outside of time. You have regressed into an aspect of your totality that is not appropriate to present circumstances, and that aspect does not have the resources to deal appropriately with current reality.

You know the experience. When you are in the grip of one of these resourceless aspects, you feel helpless, lost in the forces, and at some level, perhaps, slightly ridiculous, because you know you are capable of behaving in a more mature way. But you can't seem to get out of the clutches of the infantile level from which you are interacting with your reality.

The pattern carried in the rejected child aspect of the inner community often includes the conviction that it must do everything necessary in order not to be rejected, while at the same time knowing that whatever actions are taken won't make any difference—it will still always be rejected. Now, that may sound silly to the aspect of you that is reading this book. However, it may also sound familiar to a couple of your other aspects.

In any case, the rejected child does not know what year it is now. It does not know you have other aspects, aspects that have the resources to deal with the ups and downs of life, resources the rejected child does not have. It only knows life through the filter of rejection. Clearly, when your psyche is dominated by the rejected child, *you* don't know you have other resources, either!

You can see that being conscious of your various personal aspects is extremely useful. In any relationship, when a conflict arises that is based on the perceptions of the inner, rejected child (and you are not aware of what's happening), no clarity or maturity is possible. However, once you know your aspects and the patterns those aspects carry, you can find a new level of clarity, both in your relationships and in your life as an individual.

What are some of the common child-aspects that dominate most people's psyches? In our work, we have come across a variety of them, and we'll list those we have found to be most common. If you don't discover yourself among these examples, don't feel left out. Doing the Child Aspect Process in "Riding Lessons" will reveal your own child aspects even if they don't appear on our list. Again, remember that you don't just have an "inner child"; you have an inner kindergarten. Doing the Child Aspect Process will essentially allow you to take role-call in that inner kindergarten.

Here, then, are a few kids that may be members of the class: the Abandoned Child, the Sad Child, the Sickly Child, the Angry Child, the Lost

Child, the Angelic Child, the Rejected Child, the Deified Child, the Unloved Child, the Forgotten Child, the Bad Child, the Alien Child, the Gifted Child, the Grown-up Child, the Manipulative Child, the Stupid Child, the Adult Child, and the Innocent Child. Perhaps you can add a few of your own.

When you work with the Child Aspect Process, we recommend that you find at least four different child aspects within your inner community and then see how they show up in your daily life. As you work with your partner, you will be able to identify your inner children more and more easily when they arise in everyday situations. As you discover these members of your inner community, we recommend that you label them (Abandoned Child, Rejected Child, etc.) and that you name them as well. Giving your different aspects names is not only helpful, but it is also fun.

In the Buddhist tradition, the practice of "naming" has long been part of a technique used in meditation. While absorbed in the traditional sitting meditation, watching their breath, students are encouraged to name and label distractions as they arise in their minds. They understand that the thought-forms, the different attitudes and ideas that spontaneously arise in the mind, will then have less and less power to distract. Once they can name something, they have it rather than its having them.

Working with aspects is similar. Once you can name an aspect, you have objectified it. When you make your aspect a thing distinct from who you are, then you *have* it rather than *being* it. Naming your aspects the moment they come forward gives you awareness and a bit of distance from them. You might remember from fairy tales, myths, and magic that when you possess the name of something or someone, you have power over that thing or that person. In a way, by identifying and thereby objectifying an aspect of your psyche, you wrestle a bit of consciousness from the large body of your unconscious.

In addition to working with your child aspects, working with your adolescent aspects and bringing them to conscious awareness is useful. We all know people who still act like rebellious teenagers, though they are well past adolescence. We say they "haven't grown up," that they got stuck—and in a way that is so. They are, in fact, dominated by an aspect of their totality that is not appropriate to their chronological age or to the situations they are now in. The question then becomes: is *another* aspect available that can respond appropriately to the situation?

The adolescent stage of development is a necessary passage to move through in the process of becoming an individual. This stage gives you the opportunity to experience and create the world along the lines of your own ideas and inclinations, and to throw off many of the attitudes you learned from your parents and teachers. It is a time of creating your own identity. The purpose of youthful rebellion is to discover who you are by discovering who you are not. "Not this." "Not this." Which, hopefully, will someday lead to: "Ah, but this, yes." If one does not develop beyond the stage of rebellion, further growth and maturation are hindered. And even when we find what we can say "yes" to, we are still a long way from having developed the resources to manifest our "yes" in the world.

Most people also carry inner young adult aspects. In the young adult stage of development, the focus is on making a place for oneself in the world. Usually this is the first time young women or young men are on their own, wrestling with the demands of society, attempting to carve out a life for themselves. They are attempting to fulfill their desires and goals. This stage of life, like the two which preceded it, is dominated by the first three chakras.

As a reminder, the first three chakras are: the root chakra (at the base of the spine), the hara or second chakra (three fingers below the navel), and the third chakra (at the solar plexus). The first three chakras deal, respectively, with: (1) the physical survival of the individual, (2) procreation of the species, and (3) individual will and personal power. These three chakras are the focus of the actions and experiences of the individual during the first three stages of life (child, adolescent, and young adult). In young adulthood, when the individual begins to move out into the world, the attributes of the solar plexus are particularly important. At that time, the young adult must learn to survive in the marketplace through his or her own personal power, without the protecting (or at least, familiar) influence of the childhood home.

As with every entry into a new stage of the psyche's development, the entrance into young adulthood is an initiation into new aspects of the self. Individuals who successfully make the transition into this new stage will no longer act out unresolved adolescent issues with their parents in other areas of their life. (The adolescent aspects will still be present, of course, and can dominate the psyche whenever they are reactivated.) The young adult aspects of our psyche hold resources and patterns that earlier stages do not hold. Families are being created, babies are born, and the energy of the particular clan is being brought forward into a new generation. As with each stage, the resources are there to be embraced, integrated, and eventually released when we prepare to enter the next stage in our development.

As was true of the previous stages, we have all known individuals who cling to the young adult stage of development and do not move forward into mature adulthood. Two examples of this are: the businessman who is constantly carving out new territory, staking out his claim, in a need to prove himself in a world he perceives as the enemy; and the woman who continues to have babies simply because she has no vision of herself other than in her role as mother.

Each developmental stage of life has its corresponding aspects of consciousness. For our purposes, we define these stages as follows: conception, embryonic, fetal, infantile, child, adolescent, young adult, mature adult, elder, and death. We have come to believe that these different developmental stages—some or all of them—are established, fully formed, in the psyche at the moment of conception. The presence of the later stages of consciousness is what allows a young child to suddenly say something very wise and it accounts for the early genius of a Mozart or of a child guru. But we are also convinced that not all people carry the entire developmental sequence, and that some of the stages, in some people, may simply not be present. Individuals might only carry the stages of development up through a certain point, such as adolescence. These individuals will never move into the state of consciousness associated with the young adult, since they don't carry young adult aspects within their psyche. These individuals will either die or remain fixed at the adolescent state of consciousness, regardless of their chronological age.

When I—Rhea—was seventeen, my nineteen-year-old boyfriend hung himself on the morning of his first college exams. We had been together for four years and, though I didn't understand what was happening at the time, looking back at his struggle in the time before his suicide, I can now see that he just couldn't find in himself the resources to move from adolescence into young adulthood. He went as far as he could go but could go no farther. Ironically, his action propelled me and his seventeen-year-old brother into a maturing we had not been consciously seeking at the time. But then, perhaps that is why my unconscious put me in that situation.

Tribal cultures often provide a ritualized initiation that supports the individual in making the transition into adulthood. The onset of menstruation usually marks a shift in a female's role and position in the tribe. There may be a ritual acknowledging her entrance into womanhood, but the presence of her "blood time," signaling her ability to become a mother, is enough for her to be given the responsibilities and privileges of adulthood. For the male members of the tribe, most initiation rituals require that the "boy" access the resources of the "man" in order to survive the ritual. Since our culture doesn't practice ritual initiations that consciously attempt to open the individual to the resources of the next stage of life (the Catholic Second Communion, Protestant Confirmation, and Jewish Bar Mitzvah are but vestiges of these once powerful rituals acknowledging one's entrance into adulthood), creating one's own ritual to initiate oneself into the next developmental stage can be useful.

In addition to the transition from adolescent to young adult, another crucial developmental threshold is the one that marks the shift from mature adulthood into early elderhood. (The shift from young adulthood to mature adulthood is less clearly defined and a more gradual experience, one which seems less dramatic for most people we have observed.)

Elderhood, incidentally, is not to be confused with "old age." Rather, it is the acquisition of a level of wisdom and leadership best signaled by the broadening of one's focus beyond personal gain and accomplishment, so that it includes the welfare of the extended family or clan and also takes in community or ethnic concerns. However, fear of old age and death make this transition difficult for many of us to accept. The loss of physical prowess combined with the loss of power in our profession as we yield more and more responsibility to the younger generation is not easy—particularly for men. If a man's identity is focused solely on the power and status that can accompany mature adulthood, his letting go of that and welcoming elderhood is difficult. The inevitable loss of physical vitality adds to the difficulty. For a woman, even if she thinks she does not want children, or want any more children, a loss occurs when the opportunity to bring forth new life is no longer physically present. As with so many of life's passages, the passage into elderhood is not honored in our modern society.

Resistance to stepping into elderhood may manifest as an attempt to remain young and attractive—to hang on to our sense of vitality rather than surrendering to the next stage of life. This is the period when long-established marriages frequently break up. If the focus of the marriage was on raising a family and/or creating a place in the world, the accomplishment of these goals means that little remains to carry the couple into elderhood together. This is a time when the man may suddenly fall in love with a much younger woman, or a previously faithful wife may take a lover. If the woman has only identified with the archetype of mother, the loss of that role—demonstrated by the children leaving the nest and her inability to generate further life through her body—can present a major identity crisis. Sometimes people would rather die than make this transition—and they do.

Although in our culture, elderhood is rarely honored, people in many tribal cultures know that resources are available to elders which are valuable to the whole tribe. In such cultures, a blueprint exists for life in old age that includes the elder's having wisdom and deserving honor. Therefore, people in tribal cultures who move into this stage of development welcome rather than resist the transition.

In Hawaii, for example, one is not considered an elder until one reaches the age of eighty. To be welcomed among the other elders at that time is a great honor. We have heard of Hawaiians who actually push their age forward, saying, "I'm almost eighty," when they are only seventy-five.

In 1991, we took a group of Europeans to Hawaii on a spiritual holiday—three weeks of "holy days." We had the privilege of spending an evening with a kahuna named Sam Kihei. (A kahuna is a spiritual priest of the traditional Hawaiian culture, who may be a leader, a teacher, a healer, or a combination of the three.) Sam was a powerful presence. When he came to meet with us, it was our last night on Maui.

The people who ran the conference facility where we had been staying had given us leis of fragrant white and yellow Framijani blossoms. About forty of us, wreathed in the heady scent of the flowers, were sitting in a circle on the floor of the seminar room of the "up-country" center. Only the screens on the windows separated us from the lush vegetation that surrounded the building.

Sam entered carrying a large conch shell and wearing a beautiful brown-and-black sarong over his Bermuda shorts. He was a big man. He carried his extra weight easily and though by our standards he might have been considered fat, he was clearly at ease in his body. Sam joined our circle, sitting cross-legged with the rest of us, and gave us a greeting in the ancient Hawaiian language. Then he began his talk with us by saying, "There is no such thing as equality in traditional Hawaiian culture."

We were surprised. After all, this was America! Then he continued in his deep, rich voice: "I obey any man older than I am, and any man younger than I am obeys me. Therefore, I spend my life gathering wisdom, because I know that someday I will be the voice for my people."

Now *there* was an image of eldership that grabbed the soul. It recognized that eldership carries resources the earlier stages do not contain. It celebrated the wisdom that can develop with age and saw life as including the preparation for having the privilege of sharing wisdom with one's clan.

Our own Western culture seems to be based primarily in the adolescent and young adult stages of consciousness (with plenty of homage still given to the child levels), and the values of those early developmental stages are the ones we, as parts of that collective, tend to celebrate. Just as an individual's heroes tell us a great deal about the individual, so do a culture's heroes tell us about the culture.

Probably the best way to determine a culture's heroes is to see who receives society's highest rewards. Who, generally speaking, are the highest-paid members of our society? In America, it is the rock stars, athletes, and movie stars. Does that tell us something about the stages of human development we most honor?

In addition to the aspects that unfold sequentially, we also carry many aspects that are not tied to chronological development. However, these aspects are still parts of the personal levels of consciousness. They are still parts of individual identity. Such aspects include the Judge, the Lover, the Helper, the Parent, the Teacher, and the Criminal. Like us, you have probably seen these aspects in people of all ages.

Let's take a moment to explore the Judge, since it is particularly active in the arena of relationship. The Judge is the aspect in us that evaluates all things according to how they serve the survival of who we think we are. The

Judge makes the mistake of thinking it knows how life should be. It thinks it knows how everyone, including our partner, should be. It can be particularly specific about how we, ourselves, should be.

If you and your partner are not aware of the role the Judge attempts to play in protecting an individual's identity structure, the Judge can cause a lot of trouble. It will attempt to help other aspects of your totality avoid the emotional discomfort of your facing painful truths about yourself. It will do this by making you "right" and your partner "wrong." It will try to be sure that your self-image is not disturbed. ("It's their fault. They're to blame. Nothing is wrong with me!") The Judge's job is to maintain the identity structure called the ego, and when you are in a relationship, your ego is inevitably threatened as you and your partner surrender to the third entity that is the relationship.

Many things in a relationship threaten the ego, the most powerful of which is love. You may have noticed that after a night of deeply satisfying lovemaking with your partner, or after hours or even days of a deepening intimacy, the Judge comes back with doubled force. Suddenly all kinds of things are wrong with your partner. You feel turned-off, critical, aggressive, and/or distant. This sudden domination of the psyche by the Judge is just a way to maintain your ego structure, to maintain your separateness. The Judge is happy to provide this service. However, if you can recognize that the Judge has surfaced, you are no longer at its mercy.

When the Judge comes up, you can find a tremendous relief in just identifying what is going on instead of being sucked into the Judge's point of view. When you can *observe* the Judge, not all of you is involved in the judging and separating process. Once you have brought awareness to the situation, things begin to shift. You realize the Judge is just that—the Judge—and its voice is not necessarily the truth about your partner or about your relationship.

Once you know the Judge is dominating your inner community, you can make it an ally in your waking-up process. Since you know about projection, you know that whatever the Judge is criticizing, evaluating, or putting down is actually a part of your own unconscious material; you now have gained a powerful tool for getting to know yourself. When the Judge shows up, you can learn to pay attention—not only to what the Judge is saying about external reality but also to how what is being said relates to your own internal reality. Working with the Judge in this way allows you to use your reactivity to become conscious of what is unconsciously dominating your life.

When I—Rhea—was single, some very wise women friends told me about what they called the "black-patent-leather-shoe syndrome." It goes like this: You meet a man. He is wonderful. You fall in love. Everything is great. There is romance. There is passion. There is intimacy. And then . . . you notice that he wears black patent-leather shoes. You try to put that out of your mind and focus on how wonderful he is. As the intimacy increases, so does your attention to his black patent-leather shoes. Of course, you start thinking, "How could such a great guy wear black patent-leather shoes? How could *any* man wear black patent-leather shoes?" Then there is a little less intimacy, a little less passion, a little less romance, because . . . after all, he wears black patent-leather shoes.

Eventually, when you are with him, you can no longer focus on how wonderful he is, as you are too busy noticing his shoes. Finally *all* you can see are the shoes. And so . . . the relationship ends. After all, how could *you* be with a man who wears black patent-leather shoes . . . ?

The point of the "black-patent-leather-shoe syndrome" story is that as soon as intimacy threatens the separateness of your identity, the Judge rears its head and creates an excuse to protect the ego. For me, Gawain's "black patent-leather shoes" are his enjoyment of sex magazines. Whenever the intimacy of our relationship threatens to overwhelm my ego defenses, I find myself remembering that he likes girlie magazines. That gives me an excuse to pull back. I find myself feeling separate and aloof, because after all . . . .

What are your partner's "black patent-leather shoes"? I suggest that you identify the thing that bothers you about your partner, that keeps coming up as an annoyance, as a reason to distance yourself from him/her. Then notice what the circumstances are when you find yourself focusing on that annoying thing yet again. What does the fact that your partner wears "black patent-leather shoes" allow you to avoid? What does it allow you to justify?

As you get better at recognizing your aspects and your partner's aspects, you will be able to anticipate them. When you are able to anticipate which aspect of yours is about to surface, locating the moment of choice when you can decide which record is going to play its tune on your jukebox is easier.

You can see the hand pushing the button and, if you are centered enough in that moment, you may be able to let the moment pass without automatically playing the same old song. Or you may be able to choose to play a different record.

As we work with our partners, they will often be able to anticipate when we are about to get plugged in to one of our aspects that is not appropriate to present circumstances. When that happens, they may then be able to coach us in selecting another record before the automatic response occurs. Gawain, for example, has an aspect we call Alfred (no offense intended to those with that name), who is a real troublemaker. Alfred is rude, crude, and socially improper. He is a daredevil driver and likes to torment and tease with "games" like "how-close-to-the-ceiling-can-we-throw-the-vase-without-hitting-it."

When Alfred is about to surface, Gawain gets a particular gleam in his eyes. When Rhea sees that gleam, she knows Alfred is not far behind. If she is not in the mood to deal with Alfred, she will throw her arms over her face in mock horror and shout, "Oh, no! Not Alfred! Please! Not Alfred!" Usually we both end up laughing, and Alfred's arrival is aborted. However, remember that once the roving arm in your jukebox has picked up a particular record, there is almost no more choice and you will have to suffer through another cycle as that aspect does its thing.

We say "almost" because there *is* another possibility. If you are very alert it *is* possible to stop in the middle of one of your automatic responses . . . and center . . . and shift into a more appropriate aspect. This is difficult. It requires great awareness and commitment to consciousness. However, it *is* possible. You can, in effect, abort playing the record, even if it has already started playing. If you are alert enough to recognize the fateful tune playing on your jukebox once again, you can say: "No! Wait a minute! I am *not* listening to that one again!" You can take a breath, center, and find another aspect of your totality that is more appropriate to the moment.

The gift in becoming conscious of our personal aspects, of those aspects that are a part of our individual identity structure, is that we are then free to move beyond them. Once we are able to consciously recognize some of our personal ranges, we can begin to explore *transpersonal* ranges of consciousness. The transpersonal ranges of consciousness—which include the Divine—are as much a part of our birthright as Spirit-manifested-in-form as are the personal aspects in our individual identity system. Unfortunately, most people are unconsciously so identified with their personal aspects (and, indeed, usually with only a few of the many that are available) that they never consciously move beyond those levels into the life of the Spirit.

Although resolving personal-level issues prepares one for conscious, intentional opening to the transpersonal, sometimes the transpersonal breaks spontaneously through to the personal levels of perception and becomes conscious to the individual regardless of how much, if any, preparation has taken place. These are instances of grace. They come and go without warning or control. They are what the American psychologist Abraham Maslow called "peak experiences." These are moments we treasure, moments we recall with awe and share with those closest to us in whispered intimacy:

"The morning after my grandmother died, I woke up dreaming about her. Then I thought I heard her voice in my ear and I knew I wasn't dreaming, but I still heard her."

"I was doing my usual two-mile jog, not really thinking, because the route was so familiar, and all of a sudden I had a flash of myself sitting with my grandchildren around me and I just knew I would live a long life. Since then I haven't been nearly so fearful of dying."

"John walked in the room, but instead of seeing John's face, I saw my father's face. I somehow knew I had to call my father. When I called, I found out he had just had a heart attack and was in the hospital."

"I'd worked really hard that day and was exhausted, so I sat down to watch the sunset and rest. I was just sitting there, looking at the colors, and suddenly it occurred to me that life was a game. I mean, everything I take so seriously suddenly struck me as very funny. In that moment I knew at some level that it is all just play. I've never forgotten that experience, though I do often forget life is a game."

These moments of insight, intuition, or grace just happen. Often they seem to occur when the ordinary mind is tired or is, for some reason, out of the way. We can't make them happen; in fact, what we can say these moments have in common is that we have no control over them. That's what grace is—a gift not related to our own efforts.

However, as we clear out the unexperienced emotion that is held in the personal (usually very young) aspects of our psyche and as we become aware of our patterns, beginning to get some distance from the ego structure with which we had previously identified so closely, there is an opportunity to explore the transpersonal realms of experience more consciously and intentionally.

We would like to offer a word of caution. As you begin working on yourself and releasing your identification with the aspects that previously dominated your inner community, you will, predictably, begin moving into these realms. That is, as you begin freeing up the personal arena of your psyche, there will be space for the transpersonal to start surfacing in your experience. This can occur in many ways. Sometimes the transpersonal begins surfacing as sudden intuitions, as an abrupt "knowing" of something one has no reason to know (as we mentioned above, but on a more consistent basis). Sometimes a person may begin seeing colors or "auras" around people. Others may begin to see images that do not seem connected to physical reality yet later *are* discovered to be related—like the image of a bride moments before your friend tells you she just got engaged. Sometimes the transpersonal shows up as what seems to be a past-life memory or an ability to transmit healing energy with one's hands.

Because people do not usually know what is happening to them when these things start to occur, they can become very confused. While the East has long had systems for understanding and coping with the transpersonal realms of consciousness and their manifestations in external reality, very few roadmaps exist in the West for the spiritual journey, and Westerners are far behind in understanding these levels of experience.

We should note that Eastern models are usually based on the concept of transcendence. That is, they involve striving to transcend the personal levels of consciousness and step into the transpersonal levels, either through meditation or through induction by a guru. These techniques are ancient and are accepted as a part of the collective Eastern psyche. However, we are Westerners. We were not born into the Eastern collective. Our path as Westerners is not transcendence—rather, it is transformation.

The Eastern techniques do not export well into a Western culture. Personally, I—Rhea—feel that many of us are familiar, in terms of past lives, with the Eastern techniques and that is why they can touch us. Often, our resonance with these disciplines is very strong and we are drawn, at least for a time, into such streams once again. However, as Westerners, our path is not to jump *over* the personal into the transpersonal, but to experience the personal so completely that it naturally recedes into the background of our totality, freeing us to be open for the transpersonal to become available as such availability is appropriate to our development. That last point is extremely important: *as the availability is appropriate.* That is, one does not withdraw from life to seek the transpersonal realms. One consciously brings the transpersonal into daily life. The Eastern way is to withdraw and transcend. The Western way is to integrate and transform.

We suggest that the appeal of the Eastern approach for many Westerners is the hope that they can avoid their pain. By transcending the personal levels, they (presumably) will never have to deal with their personal pain. They will never have to take responsibility for the divergent forces that are pulling on their personal psyches, since, in the traditional Eastern disciplines, one attempts to sidestep experiencing the personal self and move right into the ocean of consciousness that is associated with the transpersonal. The possibility of taking this route can be very tempting.

One could say that the Eastern spiritual approach is to focus on the upper three chakras. Most Westerners, however, live in the demands and pulls of the lower three chakras. The path of awakening that we see as most honoring our totality as human beings is to consciously integrate the forces associated with the lower three chakras with the forces associated with the upper three chakras. The energies associated with the body and those of the spirit meet in the Heart Center. By focusing on developing our capacity to center in the heart, we do not limit ourselves to the world of form or the world of the spirit, but celebrate both as expressions of our humanity. The goal is wholeness.

Perhaps, I—Rhea—feel so strongly about preparing others for the appearance of transpersonal experiences because I had no idea what was happening when these realms started spontaneously opening to me. When I began recalling what were apparently past-life memories, I thought I was having some sort of nervous breakdown. When I began seeing colors emanating from people and I started seeing through walls, I thought something was physiologically wrong with the way my eyes connected to my brain. When I started "getting messages" and seeing the astral-level energies which some people call ghosts and spirit guides, I thought perhaps I was finally going crazy. Gradually I came to realize that these experiences were not indications that my sanity was slipping through some crack in the cosmic egg. Later I learned that they were, in fact, very predictable phases that people can pass through as they begin to free their consciousness from its conditioning and their ego begins to loosen its hold on their perception of reality.

After I went through a stage of thinking something was wrong with me, I went in the opposite direction. I passed through a stage (which, admittedly, I still find tempting) in which I thought these "special" experiences meant *I* was special. My ego wanted to claim my transpersonal experiences for its own and make me (it) different, make me special. The ego is like that, isn't it? It will use anything to enhance itself—to separate itself from others. It will even try to draw the transpersonal into the personal realm and take credit for it. Amazing! It will do anything to be in control.

If the ego finds something it cannot control, it says, "I'm in control of the fact that things happen to me that I can't control." Or, "I can't control these things. I'm just different from ordinary people." Or, "You just can't imagine the burden of being an 'old soul.' " The ego is very, very tricky. I'm sure you have met people who use their spiritual gifts to set themselves apart from others. You feel it inside yourself when you hear them interpreting your reality for you as if they are onto something you couldn't possibly understand. I cringe when I catch myself aggrandizing myself in this way, and I am sure there are many times when I do it and don't catch myself.

We all have our areas of inadequacy and will unconsciously attempt to compensate for feelings of being "less-than" in one arena by puffing ourselves up in another. The realm of spiritual prowess is not exempt from this mechanism—as when we promote so-called spiritual abilities rather than dealing with areas where we feel a lack in ourselves. We have all heard the compensation in statements like the following: "I don't really need friends. I have so many spirit guides around me that I never lack for company." Or, "I don't need orgasms because I'm just too spiritual, and besides, I see auras." Or, "I never went to college but I'm very intuitive. Who needs an education when one has tapped into the knowledge of the universe?"

If we are committed to becoming conscious, we must begin recognizing our own compensatory thoughts and actions. We have to be ruthlessly honest with ourselves. When I first began experiencing what seemed to be memories of past-lives, dazzling my friends with my "memories" was much more fun than facing the fact that I could barely pay my rent. When we hear ourselves or someone else engaging in self-promotion in one arena, we can be sure some compensation is taking place with regard to another arena.

So, if you find your ego using your emerging transpersonal experiences to serve its own needs—to diminish you ("Maybe something really *is* wrong with me"), to enhance you ("Wow! Look what I can do!"), or to compensate for areas in which you do not feel good about yourself ("Of course I'm overweight. Someone with my psychic ability needs a lot of grounding")—consider yourself the proud caretaker of a normal ego and try not to listen to it. Or, at least, try not to believe it. If you get caught up in any way with your spiritual gifts, you can become sidetracked . . . particularly because these gifts can leave as unpredictably as they came. If you identify with them ("I'm psychic!"), you have fallen into another of the ego's traps. And, in terms of your relationship, just know that as you and/or your partner begin to become more conscious, transpersonal realms may start to surface in your daily life. If you take any of it too seriously or focus on the phenomena of spiritual awakening, you may forget what the journey is really about.

The kinds of experiences cited in the above examples, in which transpersonal realms of consciousness show up in daily life, are, in general, gifts of grace. That is, they come unbidden and one has no control over their appearance—or disappearance. We mention them because such experiences have happened to us and because we have seen them happen to many of the people we work with.

It is also possible to begin consciously accessing these transpersonal ranges of your interior through the practice of meditation. If you and your partner are not already meditating together, we suggest you try it. We have found that consciously entering transpersonal levels of consciousness with your partner can add a whole new dimension to your relationship. We are very aware that, in our seminars, our work together in the transpersonal levels provides an incredible bond between us. When we are not working, we have found that meditating together is useful, so the transpersonal continues to be honored in our relationship. We notice that when we do not sit together and meditate in the morning, staying centered during the day is more difficult, and we are much more likely to get drawn into the reactivation of our child aspects. Our taking time to stop and to purposefully access the transpersonal through meditation is beneficial to us as a couple and as individuals.

At first, you may feel a bit vulnerable as you begin to access these realms with your partner. Please be assured that the transpersonal level is already present in your relationship or you would not be together. Our observation, in fact, is that such preferences of the outer mind as personal likes and dislikes have little to do with the reason we are with someone. They are "carrots" for the mind: "I like blonds" or "I love his smile" or "She's so bright" or "He's so good with his hands" or "She's got great tits." These surface preferences are just a way for the mind to be satisfied while the soul gets what it needs to come into wholeness. We are rarely aware of why we really are with our partner.

For example, when I—Rhea—was thirty-nine I fell in love with a nineteen-year-old man who had cystic fibrosis and a very uncertain future. Much to the dismay of my mother and two teenage children from my first marriage, Christopher and I were together for two years. At the end of that period, his health was stable and he was well on his way to a satisfying career. At the time I just thought I had fallen in love with a younger man. Looking back now, I see that the relationship actually served my soul as a healing.

I can see that my being with Christopher and watching him flourish was a healing of the earlier wound from the suicide of my first love. It seems as if, in being with him while he found his way, I healed myself. However, at the time I was in the relationship, I could not have seen it from that perspective.

Sometimes what the outer mind thinks it wants from a partner is not what is actually best for the soul. I—Rhea—often feel myself wanting to give Gawain my power . . . to have him tell me what to do, make decisions for me, or save me from being responsible in some area in one way or another, and he refuses to do it. (I say, "Do you think I should apologize for having said that to Jane?" He says, "What do you think?") I find that maddening—until I realize that it is only one of my child aspects speaking who wants to be saved from an embarrassing situation by "Daddy," and that my adult selves actually do prefer to take responsibility for such decisions.

Perhaps you have already seen for yourself that what you *thought* your relationship (current or past) was about turned out not to be what it was *really* about. Perhaps you've already noticed that your unconscious had its own agenda in drawing you to a partner, an agenda that was different from the ideas of your outer mind. Yet, as we move through life together, we can begin to glimpse what gifts our partner is giving us and to appreciate why we are really together.

Using the meditations in "Riding Lessons" can guide you and your partner into exploring the transpersonal ranges of consciousness and can, if you use them on a consistent basis, add an experience of depth and richness to your relationship that may previously have only appeared briefly in moments of grace.

11

SEXUALITY

Sexuality is one of the most powerful energies we all carry. This biological force, which has driven our species forward for hundreds of thousands of years, is how life maintains itself. It is impersonal and unqualified. Sexual energy is not based on morals or ethics. This force just *is*.

The essentially sexual principle of the attraction of opposites is one of the basic building blocks of the world of form. "Plus" looks for "minus," and connects. "Minus" looks for "plus," and connects. As far as modern researchers know, this force, this attraction of opposites, is present in all matter. Thus, sexual energy not only leads to the creation of organic life, but is also a dynamic that is present in all inorganic form. In human beings, the sexual force, the attraction of opposites, dictates that masculine energy is drawn toward feminine energy and will seek it out. Likewise, feminine energy is drawn toward masculine energy and will seek it out. Symbolically speaking, the north pole is attracted to the south pole, and that literally helps hold our world together.

Many of us have already discovered that love and sexuality are distinct. Though the fact may be confusing in terms of our conditioning, there can be love without sexuality and sexuality without love. To assume that love is present when sexuality is present is to assume falsely. The same holds true with regard to thinking that because you feel love toward someone, sexuality must follow. Love is not sexuality and sexuality is not love. They are distinct energies. Of course, when these two energies show up together, it is delightful.

Most of us carry a preference that love and sexual attraction go together. However, there comes a point in our development when we begin to recognize that they may not exist together. At that point, we must move beyond our preferences and open to life as it is and let go of our ideas of how it *should* be or how we *want* it to be. Instead of trying to fit life into our concepts, we must allow life to teach us what it is, rather than assuming we already know.

Most of us in the Western world have grown up in an environment strongly influenced by Judeo-Christian belief systems. Those systems, which have shaped our entire culture, carry strong beliefs, attitudes, and taboos with regard to love and sexuality. Without arguing with those belief systems, we suggest that each person must find out what works for himself or herself, and not rely on what someone else feels is an appropriate way to express life. As you open yourself to the material in this book, particularly in the highly charged areas of love and sexuality, we ask that you take in what we offer, then check out what feels right for you and follow that. As we always say in our seminars, you get to be Cinderella: if the shoe fits, it is yours.

Sexuality is present at all stages of our development, including those of infancy and elderhood. We are physical, sexual, intellectual, emotional, psychological, and spiritual Beings. All of these elements are part of our totality at all times. Sexuality does not start with puberty and end with menopause or with the entry to elderhood. It is always present—from the cradle to the grave—although, as with most natural forces, the sexual energy within any individual ebbs and flows. Additionally, sexual energy clearly plays a stronger role for some individuals than it does for others, just as patterns that emphasize the intellect or physical strength may also be stronger for some. However, that force we call sexuality is present, as a part of who we are, throughout our life. This is useful to remember in our attempts to understand ourselves and others.

Babies have sexual energy, and babies are also bound by the natural law of the attraction of opposites. This means they are attracted to the parent of the opposite gender. A little girl is attracted sexually to her father. A little boy is attracted sexually to his mother. Thus, our sexuality is first activated when we are infants, by the presence of the countergender forces in our parents or caretakers. The countergender parent represents the first time the north pole gets an experience of the south pole.

To be more accurate, our countergender parent represents the first screen onto which we project our own inner, countergender aspects. As females, we project our own masculine aspects onto the screen our father provides for us. As males, we do the same—projecting our own inner feminine aspects onto our mother. The rest of life is an attempt to reclaim and unite our own inner male and female. We will use many different individuals as screens for our inner countergender aspects throughout our lifetime. We will do so in an attempt to know ourselves. And as we come to know ourselves through our partner, we will, with wisdom, begin to reclaim our other half—our own countergender aspects—to take back our projections and move toward wholeness.

The myths and folk tales that speak about the long-ago split of one's soul into two parts and the subsequent search for the "other half" are based on this truth. We project our "other half" outward onto the screen of external reality and spend the rest of our life searching for the experience of wholeness we feel will come when we reunite with our "soul mate."

It is an accurate impulse. We are whole when we cease unconsciously projecting our own inner countergender aspects—our anima or animus, as Jung would have said—onto the screens of external reality. If you and your partner both have this awareness, you can consciously use your relationship to take back your projections and move toward the experience of personal wholeness.

This possibility is yours for the claiming. It is not dependent on some trick of fate which happens to place your soul mate on your path in this lifetime. Seen from this perspective, all members of the opposite sex represent our "soul mates." That is, they represent aspects of ourselves we have projected outward onto the screen of external reality. What we like and what we dislike in our partner are really aspects of ourselves that we have projected outward onto them. As we begin to take back our projections, we start to see more of our own totality. We move toward wholeness. "Ah ha! This, too, is me!" Once we start to take back our projections, and only then, do we begin to have the opportunity to see who our partner really is.

Perhaps you have heard it said that we marry our parents. Usually, at least in the first marriage, we do seem to marry our countergender parent. Thus, we might more accurately say that we project our own unconscious countergender aspects onto the closest countergender screen we can find. First we project our own countergender aspects onto our parents, then onto our mates, and eventually onto our countergender children. With the projection comes the longing for union, the longing to reclaim our "other half." Sexual attraction is part of the longing for wholeness.

Even though the existence of an attraction to the parent of the opposite sex is clearly recognized by modern psychology, most of us still have difficulty acknowledging that this attraction exists within us. And yet, this is how sexuality is passed from one generation to another. The attraction to the countergender parent is part of the pattern that helps preserve our species. The little girl wants Daddy, but because of the presence of Mommy and of our social taboos, she can't have Daddy. So, when she is old enough, she transfers her (usually unconscious) desire for Daddy to a peer and procreates. She will later transfer this sexual attraction to her son and, through the presence of that sexual energy, will induct her son into his own sexuality. The son is attracted (again, usually unconsciously) to the mother. He can't have her because Daddy is there (and he is bigger and stronger), so when the son is old enough, that energy gets transferred to a woman who is available . . . and the species continues. When he later becomes the father of a daughter, the sexual attraction is transferred to the daughter, which in turn initiates the little girl into her sexuality. In this way, the wave of sexuality moves through the generations. It is natural. It has always been so. The myths of Oedipus and Electra are "myths" precisely because they speak of something basic in the human collective.

Because children as well as adults have conscious and unconscious sexual feelings, children as well as adults can be actively involved in creating and carrying through instances of sexual interaction, not only with other children but also with adults, even though the latter instances may be forbidden by taboo or law or common sense. Thus, children, when they are approached by adults for or engaged by adults in sexual activities, are not innocent victims. They play their part, consciously or unconsciously, in drawing those experiences to themselves.

Clearly, a child is not meant to act out its sexuality with an adult. It has neither the physical nor the emotional capacity to deal with sexual activity with an adult. A child does not have the resources to deal with the tremendous forces unleashed through active sexual interaction with an adult, and engaging these forces prematurely is overwhelming to the child's psyche. Sexual activity with an adult is not appropriate to the child's stage of development. The psychic wound that is generated when these forces are engaged by a child often takes decades to resolve. So, please be clear that we are in no way advocating or excusing sex with children. At the same time, we suggest that the presence of sexual energy in a child is natural. We would also like to suggest that there are no victims—not really.

If the totality of who you are orchestrated your reality so you had an experience of incest or sexual molestation as a child, it did so for a reason. If you look, *after* you have released the pain and the confused emotions connected to the experience, you will see that the wound also holds a gift. Something happened for you as a result of that experience that would not have happened if had it not occurred. Some resources were developed within you that would not otherwise have been yours. Again, we are not suggesting that your conscious personality set up the incident. However, some part of your totality did. We are not suggesting blame or guilt. We are suggesting responsibility. We are suggesting the possibility of redeeming that experience through the knowledge of how it has served.

What we often see in people with whom we work in our seminars is that those who experienced early sexual abuse usually have a great deal of sexual energy. The presence of so much sexual energy can be quite overwhelming and confusing for children. Often the incident involving sexual abuse gives them a psychological reason to suppress their sexual energy and then to direct their attention to developing other aspects of their totality—often their spirituality. Perhaps it is because of the spiritual orientation of our groups that we often see individuals who have strong spiritual gifts and yet have not owned, or are not yet comfortable with, their sexuality. Some people are drawn into the abstract forms of spirituality that focus on theory and belief systems as an escape from the body and its mysterious demands. They are drawn to the upper three chakras as a refuge from the difficult-to-control energies of the lower three chakras; drawn to the masculine virtues of the illumined mind as a defense against the chaotic feminine forces associated with the body and the earth.

We have often found among participants in our seminars that the opportunity to develop spiritually was based on the repression of sexuality, and *that* was triggered by a traumatic sexual experience. Many times they do not consciously remember the traumatic sexual experience. As we have said, the child has no resources to deal with the overwhelming forces associated

95

with adult sexuality, so the child's psyche may protect him or her by repressing the traumatic memory—which means the emotions and the sexual energy associated with that memory are also repressed. When individuals are older and do have the resources to deal with their sexual energy without being overwhelmed, the memories of the abuse may begin to surface. So, if you are reading an article about incest or watching a TV program about child molestation and your own memories of abuse suddenly start coming to consciousness, it is a sign that you are now ready to deal more completely with your own sexual energy.

Many people think the surfacing of such memories is a sexual setback. Actually, the opposite is true. Rose Kennedy wisely said, "God never gives you anything you can't handle." We'd like to paraphrase her statement to read, "Your psyche never gives you anything you can't handle." The surfacing of any traumatic memory is an indication that you are now ready to handle the forces connected to the memory. Your inner wisdom is decreeing that you now have resources you previously lacked. That is why what was repressed is now available to your consciousness. We suggest that you take it as an acknowledgment that can empower you, rather than as a setback that can diminish you.

If you look honestly at an incest experience with your own countergender parent, you may see that some aspects of your totality either enjoyed it or, at the least, wanted it. That is not to say other aspects of your inner community did not have quite different responses. However, as we move into adulthood, we see that nothing is simple. Nothing is black or white. The horror of incest is true *and* the attraction is true. The presence of the unconscious attraction is the source of the guilt that many children experience with regard to an incestuous incident. But the presence of a very natural attraction is not blameworthy. To suggest that the child's own sexual energy was involved in an incident of incest is not to say it was the child's "fault" the incident occurred.

We have met people in our groups who have a feeling that they might have been sexually abused or who have vague memories of sexual abuse. As we have looked deeper into these feelings and vague memories, it has become clear that while no actual incident of incest may have occurred, the presence of sexual energy between the child and the adult took symbolic form as a "memory," as if an incident *had* occurred. We feel this is one explanation for the growing evidence that not all "memories" of abuse stem from actual physical events.

If, as a parent, you have experienced a sexual attraction to your children, it is not bad. While acting out that sexual attraction is not appropriate, such an attraction is natural. Usually, however, we don't even allow ourselves to acknowledge the presence of a sexual attraction to our children. Again, however: what we resist, persists. If you acknowledge the presence of a sexual attraction to your children (or to another child), you create the opportunity for that energy to shift internally and even to transform. If you repress the awareness of the attraction, you are actually much more likely to act on it, either overtly or covertly, through obsessive attachment to the child or excessive physical contact that manages to stay just within what is acceptable. We know a family where the mother takes showers with her twelve-year-old son and another where the thirteen-year-old daughter replaces her mother in her father's bed when the mother is traveling. While these are not instances of incest, some unconscious sexual dynamic is clearly at play.

A couple of years ago, I—Rhea—realized that I was, yet again, resisting going deeper into my love for Gawain. When I looked at the source of that resistance, I was shocked. I discovered that one or more of my infantile and/or child aspects was still "saving herself for Daddy." My parents divorced when I was a year and a half old and a couple of the younger members of my inner community were still hoping Daddy would come back. They reasoned that if they allowed me to give myself fully to another man, I/they wouldn't be available when Daddy finally showed up. They had been waiting, protecting my heart, as it were, for almost half a century. Since that was the hope of "their" life, "they" felt as if my giving myself fully to Gawain would kill "them." I had to consciously allow them their grief.

As we mentioned in the section on working with your aspects, it is often useful to communicate with those aspects of your inner community that have not been heard. So I talked to these newly discovered parts of myself and tried to acquaint them with current reality. I assured them that Daddy wasn't ever going to show up. I felt those aspects mourning with me for two days. Finally, almost viscerally, I could feel them recede into the background of my psyche. A new level of intimacy and connectedness with Gawain followed.

Our countergender parent provides us with our first blueprint of the opposite sex, leading to the development of feelings which we then, if our development is relatively healthy, transfer onto our adult partner. However, people don't recognize that often the sexual relationship they experience with their partner is unconsciously incest-based. Before a woman begins to wake up, all men are, to some degree, unconsciously her father. Likewise, for a man, before he becomes conscious of this dynamic, all women are, at some level of his psyche, unconsciously his mother. For people who have never owned their attraction to their parent of the opposite sex, being clear and conscious in their relationship with their mate is difficult.

We have observed that when, through their mate, people are unconsciously making love to their parent, society's taboos enter the sexual relationship. This may manifest as a feeling that they have to hide something about their sex life or simply as a withholding of the fullness of their sexual energy. What they are actually trying to hide, or to withhold from their consciousness, is the incestuous attraction they carry for their countergender parent. No matter how attractive that parent was or was not, no matter how much they approved or disapproved of that parent as a person, the attraction is still there. We hide this from ourselves as well as unconsciously attempting to hide it from others. (Please note: if you have a strong reaction to what is written here, if you feel yourself getting reactivated, you can be sure that some of your own unconscious incestuous feelings are getting touched. Otherwise, why would it disturb you?)

One way to confront the issue of sexual attraction for the countergender parent and to probe your own psyche on the issue is sexual role-playing. With your partner, you can experience the sexual act as if your partner were the countergender parent. That means, if you are a woman, you set things up with your partner so he plays the role of Daddy, and you make love to him. Or he makes love to you as if you were his little girl. For a man, have your wife or girlfriend act out the role of Mother in the sexual act and see what happens. Almost unfailingly, this will set all kinds of experiences in motion. For same-sex relationships, making love with your partner as if he/she were the parent of the same sex could likewise be very revealing.

Perhaps the thought of making love to your parent, as played by your partner, revolts you. Perhaps you feel shy about it, or embarrassed. Perhaps it turns you on. Perhaps you will get angry or become depressed. Perhaps, as you are attempting this role-playing, you freeze up and can't continue. Perhaps it will feel so ridiculous to you that you crack up laughing. Whatever your reaction may be, notice it and go through with the process anyway. More likely than not, the process will set free an amazing amount of energy.

So much energy is held in our unconscious attraction to the countergender parent that, unless it is somehow freed, the experience of sexuality with our partner stays limited. One way the unconscious attraction to the countergender parent may manifest in relationship is in the tendency to perceive our partner as either a saint or a sinner. This is the basis of the so-called Madonna/whore syndrome. Men have a tendency to perceive their wives as the Madonna, and the range of sexuality they allow themselves to experience with their wives is limited to that image. If you are unconsciously attracted to your mother (the Madonna) and choose your partner within the parameters of how similar she is to your mother, then once you marry her, or she becomes your partner, in the simplicity of your psyche, she becomes your mother—and you must not fuck your mother. No matter how good the experience of sexuality might have been originally, once the transference of the mother image onto the partner has deepened, the sexuality will likely shift within the parameters allowed by the mother image. Sooner or later, you will have to find somebody else—the whore—to have hot, passionate sex with, because that kind of sexual experience is taboo with your mother, who is now represented by your partner. The same dynamic exists for a woman in relation to her unconscious desire for her father, which then gets transferred to her mate.

The attraction of opposites dominates our sexual relationships. This applies to gay and lesbian couples as well as heterosexual couples. Masculine is attracted to feminine and vice versa, regardless of the gender of the physical body. From the standpoint of the psyche, there is no such thing as a "homo" sexual relationship. The north pole is not attracted to the north pole. The north pole is attracted to the south pole.

We are multiple beings, with both masculine and feminine aspects within us, regardless of our outer sexual gender. The outer levels are basically superficial. Thus, what is at play in the attraction is the essential energy of the individual. When the masculine aspects of one man are attracted to feminine aspects within another man, or his own inner feminine is attracted to the masculine aspects of another man, and those aspects enter a sexual relationship, we call the relationship "homosexual." The same goes for "lesbian" women, in which a feminine aspect in one woman is attracted by the masculine aspect in another woman.

Now, take a breath—this next part could be a tough one. While the idea may be a stretch, there is value in our recognizing that since each of us has both masculine and feminine aspects, we are all also homosexual. That is to say, for each of us there will be times in life when we are sexually attracted to someone of our own external sexual gender. This is natural.

As a woman, your inner masculine aspects may be sexually attracted to the feminine aspects in another woman. I—Rhea—remember relationships with girlfriends, particularly when I was younger, where the dynamics of the relationship included jealousy, possessiveness, and easily hurt feelings that were more like what might be found in a tempestuous romance than in a simple friendship . . . and yet there was no overt sexuality in the relationships. And is all that butt slapping and locker-room humor among males really without a sexual component? Since we are multiple, a man may be sexually attracted to the feminine aspects in another man, although that attraction may never be conscious. However, if the unconscious attraction to a person of the same external gender does become conscious, it does not mean we now need to identify ourselves as gay.

In our seminars, we have seen many people who either spend a great deal of energy denying the presence of such energy, or who, in recognizing the presence of a sexual attraction to a person of the same gender, suddenly think it means they need to act upon that attraction and/or lead a homosexual or lesbian lifestyle. But they do not need to. We are multiple beings with many different aspects. We have within us both male and female aspects, and those aspects will be attracted to the opposite gender wherever they find it.

Since you—along with everyone else—carry both masculine and feminine aspects in your totality, you can consider it to be a gift in an intimate relationship when your male aspects are attracted to your partner's female aspects and your female aspects are attracted to your partner's male aspects . . . regardless of your own external gender or your partner's. When one partner's inner feminine aspects are attracted to the other partner's inner masculine aspects, and vice versa, the richness of the relationship increases.

Remember the old saying, "It's easy to see that she wears the pants in the family"? We all know relationships in which the woman carries most of the masculine energy and the man is essentially feminine in nature, though the relationship is clearly heterosexual. As we open to our own multiplicity, we can also consciously open to the multiplicity of our partner. We can consciously move about in our own inner community and create the opportunity for our partner also to shift from one aspect to another. This can give the un-lived aspects of the psyche a chance to express themselves.

Once when we were staying in a very fancy hotel in Hamburg, Germany, I—Rhea—surreptitiously put my sexiest underwear on beneath what I had been wearing and told Gawain I was going shopping. I took the elevator downstairs and called him from the lobby. When he answered, I began in a sultry voice: "I understand your wife is out for a while . . . . " That afternoon the latent call-girl aspect of my psyche had a great time!

If we are willing to open to the vulnerability and the intimacy of sexual role-playing with our partner, we can mutually enter into endless games and countless areas of exploration. "Okay, Honey. Tonight I want to play whore." Or, perhaps more threatening, "I'd like you to be my father and fuck my brains out." By role-playing with your partner, you can bring to consciousness many of the unconscious sexual dynamics between you and your countergender parent. Not only will you release a lot of withheld energy, but you can also expand the range of sexuality that is now allowable with your partner. Furthermore, you do not need to look outside your relationship to satisfy those aspects of your own sexuality that don't fall within the "Okay with Mom [or Dad]" limitation. Also, your partner is released from the need to be a saint for you and can act out wider ranges of sexuality than the ones you previously and unconsciously allowed her or him to act out in the relationship.

As you free each other, you free a great deal of unconscious, bound-up energy. That energy is now available to deepen and enrich your relationship with each other. This touches the same principle we discussed in the section on secrets—anything you hold back from your partner limits the depth of intimacy you can experience in your relationship. Whatever you attempt to hide or hold back (from your partner or yourself) translates into energy that is unavailable for your union and for life.

In your relationship, acknowledging what is true for you in the sexual arena is important, even if it carries a societal taboo. The Secret Process in "Riding Lessons" is an invaluable aid in probing this area. For example, acknowledging to your partner what turns you on sexually can lead to a wonderfully fun and lust-filled experience.

Most of us have to press through some shyness or embarrassment, and experience some vulnerability, in order to share honestly our hidden sexual thoughts. Some aspects of our inner community would rather do anything than reveal our sexual secrets, fantasies, and unspoken desires.

Perhaps you have always wanted to experiment with a certain sexual position. Perhaps you would like to experience being dominated or playing sex-slave. Perhaps you secretly hold a desire to be raped. Perhaps you are drawn to S&M. Perhaps a transvestite is hiding inside you and is longing to be acknowledged. Perhaps you have fantasies about group sex or desire a particular technique of oral sex or anal sex. Whatever it may be, just acknowledge that it's true for you. Or, better said, acknowledge what is true for the aspect who is doing the sharing at that moment. Some of your aspects may be shocked by the sexual preferences or curiosities of some of your other aspects. Again, remember that what we resist persists, and that we are multiple, not singular.

Because of your own inner Judge, or other dominant aspects of your inner community which seem to be (or actually are) socially acceptable, some of your socially unacceptable aspects may never have been given a voice. Can you imagine all the energy that's required to hide those aspects of your interior from your partner and from yourself? All that energy is then not available to you in your life. When you use your life-force to suppress yourself, to withhold your truth, you affect your health and your overall well-being—and you definitely affect your relationship. If you can press through your inhibitions and any lingering social taboos and tell your partner what is going on with you about sex, then the two of you can choose, if you wish, to dramatize anything you have shared. You may not need to act out everything you share, though. Often, just finally saying what has been in your thoughts is sufficient.

102

Individually and collectively, all our rules and proscriptions about sex are based in our attempt to control its incredible power. It is a power that cannot be denied, though the outer mind is often humiliated by the existence of a force it cannot easily control—particularly if that force is associated with the body.

The mind/body split is older than Apollo and Dionysus. We all carry it. It is part of our collective conscious and unconscious nature. The fact that you are reading this book no doubt means the time has come for you to confront this split within your own psyche. Only by embracing your sexuality *and* your spirituality can you go deeper into who and what you really are. Discovering and peeling off the more superficial layers of yourself in the arena of sexuality can be a delight and it will definitely deepen your capacity to experience intimacy in your relationship.

12

LOVE

When love beckons to you follow him,
Though his ways are hard and steep.
And when his wings enfold you yield to him,
Though the sword hidden among his pinions may wound you.
And when he speaks to you believe in him,
Though his voice may shatter your dreams as the north wind lays
waste the garden.

–Kahlil Gibran, *The Prophet*

We believe the energy, the mysterious force, which lies behind the word "love" is what holds the universe together. All manifestations are expressions of that one force. Everything is an offshoot or mutation of that one energy. Underneath all expressions of life, even those that initially appear to be evil, there is only one energy, one force—and that force can be called love. Our striving, our desires, and our actions are all expressions of love, no matter how separate from love they may appear to be.

In a relationship, the patterns of interaction and behavior are connected to love regardless of whether they seem to be or not. Love is the substance of our relatedness, even when that love is distorted to the point of appearing to be its opposite. If we could peel away the layers of an outer manifestation that expresses itself as hostility or cruelty, we would eventually find either love or resistance to the pain associated with love. Underneath everything, we will find the energy that we call love.

While all of us may, at moments in our lives, have caught glimpses of the truth that "everything is love," we do not generally live our daily lives out of that realization. If we did, life on this planet would look very different.

And since we don't live in the constant awareness of the love that lies underneath all of our activities, we get caught in the many illusions that mask the mystery called love. Because of this, we can find value in delving into some of the manifestations of love and becoming a bit clearer about various of the masks behind which the energy called love hides.

Having as many different words for "love" as the Eskimo has for "snow" would be nice. But, alas, we are limited to one word for the experience "love." Therein lies the source of much confusion and ambiguity in our attempts to identify and verbalize our inner reality. We struggle for clarity by adding qualifiers: brotherly love, romantic love, patriotic love, divine love, etc. In the chapter on the Heart Center, for example, we talked about unconditional love—love that is not tied to preferences and prejudices, love that simply is. That love is the source of the "hum" beneath all manifestation. We have all heard that hum, however briefly. Nevertheless, despite our attempts at clarity, things get murky the moment the "l-word" is used.

In order to move toward clarity about love in our discussion of relationship, recalling once again that we are multiple Beings is useful. Our different aspects experience love differently. What our inner children experience as love is very different from the experience of love by our mature and/or elder aspects. In a relationship, therefore, we can ask ourselves *which* aspects of our own inner community are "in love" with our partner and which are not. (Certainly not all of our aspects are in love with our partner, nor are all of our aspects even thrilled about being in relationship.)

In intimate relationships, being aware of how our inner children see and experience love is particularly important. Because most people are unaware that different and distinct aspects even exist within their psyche, they never question the different and often conflicting beliefs about and experiences of love they carry. Hence, in their relationships, they often fail to recognize that what is driving them and often creating immense suffering is coming from the children in their inner community, not from the adults. Therefore, we will spend some time considering the infantile and childish aspects of the psyche with regard to love.

We suggest that for the infantile and child aspects of the psyche, little distinction exists between *love* and *attention*. The child is needy. It needs someone around to take care of it. Since it is literally helpless and unable to survive on its own in the early stages of life, it is *completely* dependent on others for survival. In order to get what it needs, in order to survive, it has to attract attention. It must make its environment aware of itself and of its needs. The child feels it cannot survive without attention. So it finds ways to attract attention.

The very young child may scream or cry in order to be noticed. That is probably the reason life gave babies their ability to create such a penetrating noise. Later, as the child grows, it develops different strategies to attract attention. Some children whine and complain, others get sick, others become performers, some become "good" little boys or girls, while others get attention by being "bad."

In the process of awakening, becoming aware of what techniques our own inner children have developed in order to attract attention is essential. These techniques or strategies are part of our inner patterning and will persist in coming into expression throughout our lifetime. That is, the children in our inner community will *continue* to use the strategies they used in childhood to get attention, even though we are now adults. And when those children get that attention, they will experience being loved. Likewise, if they do not get attention using the familiar ploys, they will experience not being loved.

When I—Rhea—was a child, one of the ways I attracted attention was by getting sick. My mother or grandmother would stay home from work and take care of me. I interpreted this as an expression of love. When Gawain gets sick, however, he just wants to be left alone. This is very hard for me, since some part of me still experiences being sick as an opportunity to give and receive love. My tendency is to fuss over him as an expression of my love for him, whereas for him, an expression of love involves my leaving him alone. (An exercise in the "Riding Lessons" section that will support you in discovering these areas of your own relationship is "How Do You Say 'I Love You'?")

Let's look at one, perhaps familiar way the inner children influence apparently adult relationships. Have you ever wondered why the threat of the loss of a lover is such a painful experience? Sometimes our reactions to the possibility that a partner might fall in love with someone else and/or leave us is so strong that we feel as though *we are going to die, that we will not survive*. Capable, self-reliant, resource-filled adults will often experience terror at the mere thought that their lover might suddenly express an interest in someone else, or leave, or die. Although a feeling of fear in such circumstances is appropriate, we suggest that the overwhelming power of some of the emotions that surface under these conditions, or even in the face of the possibility that these conditions could occur, is a function of the part of us that hasn't realized we are no longer two years old. No matter how many times our friends tell us "there are other fish in the sea," we feel annihilated. This feeling comes from the inner children whose *physical* survival was dependent on the attention and presence of the Other.

For many people, the strong physical reaction associated with the threat or the fear of being abandoned by the beloved can dominate the whole relationship. Many of us will do anything to avoid the experience of being abandoned or of having the loved one leave. Some people even become the abandoner as a defense against the possibility of having to experience being abandoned. In effect, they are saying, "I'll leave you before you can leave me."

Further, if you carry an abandoned child in your inner kindergarten, you are likely to continue creating circumstances in which you are "abandoned." If the abandoned child is dominating your psyche, it will *need* to create abandonment in order to maintain its identity. That is who it is. That is how it stays "alive." Without abandonment, there is no existence. This is another reason why beginning to recognize the aspects you carry and becoming conscious of which aspect is dominating your experience of life is so useful.

In an adult/adult relationship, you may still be using the techniques you used as a child to get attention, and then experiencing that attention as love. For example, if you got attention as a child by becoming sick and having accidents, you are likely to find a partner who (at least initially) loves to take care of people, someone who gains his/her identity by being a helper. If you are the performer type, you will invariably attract someone who will (at least initially) admire your performing and, in this way, support your pattern in the same way your parents did. If you have a good-little-girl/boy pattern, it will attract either another "good" girl/boy (which generally is initially comforting and eventually boring) or a partner who carries a "bad" girl/boy pattern, who will dramatize your shadow for you (which generally is initially exciting and eventually tumultuous). Since the psyche strives for wholeness, a pattern which complements *your* patterns will appear somewhere in your life to balance your energies—if not in your partner, then in the people around you. We will go into this mechanism further in the section on patterns and shadows.

Since love and attention are essentially equivalent for your inner children, your recognizing the strategies you use to get attention will support you in understanding how you relate to those you love. Then, as you become aware of the strategies and patterns of your inner infants and children, you maximize the possibility of becoming more conscious in your relationships. The Child Aspect Processes in "Riding Lessons" can help you discover the strategies your particular inner children use to get attention.

We have all seen and/or lived in relationships that are abusive. The classic response of the abused wife when asked why she doesn't leave her husband is, "I know he really loves me." Again, for the inner children, love is attention; it is survival. Any attention is perceived as love. Negative or abusive attention is perceived by our inner children as love if that is how we received attention as children. Attention (perceived as love) that is expressed as abusive behavior and violence will now be preferred by those inner children to no attention, meaning "no love." Through this equating of love/attention and abuse, some part of the psyche thinks it *needs* abuse in order to survive, and will unconsciously seek it out. The child feels it must have abuse in order to survive physically and the adult now feels (usually unconsciously) he/she must have abuse to survive psychologically. If you carry this pattern and if you allow your psyche to be dominated by your inner children, you will create abuse as a way to experience attention/love. In other words, you will create many personal, energy-draining "dramas" unless you can distinguish between the psychological survival of the inner children and the experience of mature love.

Clearly, the same is true for those of us who experienced love/attention as violence. Our inner children interpreted the intensity of the attention we received when our parents were violent with us as love, and so those inner children will only feel "love" when the intense attention they are accustomed to—i.e., violence—is present.

A major question is: what happens when the resources of your adult aspects are used to fulfill the needs or desires of your inner children? If one of your child aspects feels you really need something, particularly if that part of you thinks you can't survive without it, you will, either consciously or unconsciously, use all of your skill to get it. The mind of the child isn't developed enough to be especially subtle and clever in its attempts to use manipulation to get what it wants. However, the adult mind is. Unless the individual is aware, the inner infants and children will use the individual's adult skills in service to those immature inner aspects. This shows up most often in the individual's love relationships.

Let us recapitulate. The child is needy. It needs attention from its parents or whoever is around to take care of its survival requirements. Attention is the main quality connected to its survival. Once attention is given, a basic need is filled, even if the attention is so-called negative attention, in the form of violence or abuse. So, in all deep relationships, your inner children will unconsciously activate your particular scheme for getting attention from your partner and regard the experience of getting that attention as "love." Since the infantile aspects think you need attention in order to survive, you will use your adult skills to get this attention. When the need for attention is met, a basic, unconscious fear for your survival is, at least temporarily, alleviated. This momentary relaxation, this momentary release of the unconscious fear, then becomes the experience you seek. (Remember, the attention-getting mechanism we are talking about exists within only a part of your totality. We are not talking about something that applies to all of your aspects. For those very young aspects of the inner community, however, life is about attempting to get love/attention so they can feel safe.)

To those of us who are just beginning to wrestle consciously with the mystery of being human, life seems to be something that is *happening to us* rather than something that *flows through us*. Therefore, the relief we experience by having someone give us attention/love seems to be created by the Other. Since your parents, your partner, your teachers, or your guru seem thus to be the source of your experience, you need to get what you want *from* them. You will, usually unconsciously, use your old strategies—first to get and then to continue getting this love/attention—to avoid the fear associated with not getting attention. This mechanism in relationship sets up an exhausting series of predictable interactions that conceal a deeper, frenetic dance to get the Other to give you what you feel you need. Perhaps this process is familiar to you.

If you don't get what you think you need from other people, you may try harder to manipulate them into providing what you think you need. You may try to make them feel guilty because they didn't give you what you want; they didn't grant you the experience you associate with being loved. If that doesn't work, if that doesn't get them to behave in a way that relaxes your inner tension, you will start to resent them and make them wrong. Often you will unconsciously start a fight that really has little to do with what it seems to be about on the surface. You really just want to make them wrong for not rescuing you from the tension you are experiencing. Sound familiar? This mechanism is at the core of a lot of suffering between partners. As with other mechanisms, though, once you are conscious of its presence, the possibility exists that you can step beyond it. Discovering that you are no longer two years old and that you have resources at your disposal you did not have as a child is particularly useful. As a resource-filled adult, you have many other ways to experience love than simply by getting attention.

As you get to know your inner community, you can discover which child aspect is the most dominant in your experience of love. Finding that out can provide the "Ah-ha" which allows you to begin making your unconscious mechanisms conscious. Such clarity and consciousness will shift the way you experience your relationships. Then you will have a much greater chance to experience mature love in an adult relationship.

As you consciously shift into your adult aspects while exploring the mystery of love, you go deeper and deeper into yourself. You begin to experience love as something that flows *through* you rather than something you need to have come *to* you. Gradually you discover that love is a natural expression of your essence. In the end, you discover that the source of love lies within you and not outside of you.

Remember the time, or times, when you fell in love? Much like the overture to romantic classical music touches on themes that will later be elaborated, the themes that appear when you first fall in love will later develop into the issues and the qualities that define the relationship.

Everything is present from the beginning. From the start, we have glimpses of the themes that will later become dominant forces in the relationship. Usually, when we first fall in love, we feel great. We notice the birds singing, the sky seems blue even if it is gray, we seem to float through the air, and we are happy—at one with ourselves and the world. It is not difficult to understand that some people fall in love with the experience of falling in love.

What really occurs when you "fall in love"? The *apparent* facts are that you (finally!) have the experience of someone accepting and even celebrating you just the way you are, and it feels wonderful. That experience suspends, for a while, the belief most of us carry, which is that we are not lovable. It is as if, for a time, you are free from the confinement of all the old beliefs and attitudes you have about yourself. You feel free and wonderful. But is this what is *really* happening? Perhaps something else is going on, which accounts for the intensity of being "in love." What really happens is that you briefly project onto the beloved the part of yourself that loves you and, through that person, you are able to experience your own self-love.

After a while that feeling fades. Your own inner mechanisms, the old beliefs that you are not lovable, will begin to dominate your experience once again. When that happens, your experience of "the beloved" changes. He or she starts to find things wrong with you. Small things that, though glimpsed briefly, were not worth mentioning during the honeymoon phase suddenly become important. Little things become issues and those issues are then used as evidence that "this relationship isn't working." You are falling out of love.

What has really happened is that the aspects inside you which believe you are not lovable are coming back to the forefront. In the face of the resurgence of those aspects, you are not able to sustain the projection onto the Other of your feelings of "the beloved." Instead, those aspects of your own psyche that are critical of you, that judge you and are never satisfied, come forward once again and are projected onto the Other. Naturally, your perception of the Other changes as this inner shift occurs. However, you can only recognize what is really happening if you realize that the outer relationship is an expression of your own inner drama, which is then projected onto an outer screen called the Other. Nobody is really "out there" doing anything to you. When you recognize this, you are confronted with your own capacity—or lack thereof—for self-love.

Once you recognize that your relationship with the external "beloved" is an expression of your internal relationship to the "beloved" who is yourself, though your relationship seems to be getting sour or the love that seemed so abundant seems to be disappearing, you can ask yourself this question: "Who is it that is *not* loving me?" If you look deep enough, you will discover that some members of your own inner community are not loving other aspects. If you can understand this mechanism, catch what's going on, and consciously shift back into the aspects that are in touch with your self-love, you will immediately perceive that shift as being reflected by your partner. This is another way you can use your relationship for self-discovery.

The mature aspects of the psyche are able to love the Other as a unique expression of the life force. The mature aspects of the psyche recognize that their survival is not dependent upon the Other and hence that no need exists to manipulate the Other into certain ways of being or behaving. The dependence of the child aspects of the psyche and the need for independence by the adolescent aspects are, in mature stages, replaced by an acknowledgment of the interdependence that exists when a partnership is dedicated to the fulfillment of both individuals. Mature love is able to move beyond the infant/child association of love with attention. Mature love can delay the gratification of needs and desires and carry the tension of delaying them until their fulfillment is appropriate for all concerned.

Mature love is, in its fullness, a great mystery. Once you are initiated into its powers, it will carry you into a deeper and deeper vortex of energies and experiences over which you have little power and no control. As you open to mature love, there is a pull to surrender consciously to the mystery that is unfolding rather than an attempt to protect yourself through control. New ways of being begin to present themselves. You find a willingness to "melt" with the Other, a willingness that has the capacity to short-circuit your ego and connect you directly to your essence. Through the process of an ever-deepening intimacy with your partner, you will be able to connect more and more deeply with your own essence, as your partner mirrors that essence for you.

Of course, as your essence is reached . . . as you are, as Gibran says, wounded by the sword of love, all the old pain associated with love, the pain you have not dealt with, will begin to surface. And you, like most of us, would probably rather run from love than feel that pain. In the ever-deepening intimacy of your relationship, all the reasons why you closed off love in the first place will confront you. As you open your heart, the first things you will encounter are the reasons you closed your heart originally. Whether you embrace the pain as an opportunity for growth and awareness or flee from the pain by leaving the relationship or by attempting to keep the relationship superficial is between you and your soul.

If you choose to use your relationship as a path to awareness, step by step you will discover that you are returned to your own essence. By giving up your projections and your defenses with regard to the Other, you can, in moments of grace, become aware that you *are* the Other. The essence in you is the same essence that is in your partner. In fact, on that fundamental level, you can experience that you and the Other are one. From such a place, you can expand to experience that your essence, your partner's essence, and the essence of Life are one. Who you are is the energy of love incarnate and what you see around you is, in fact, an internal drama projected out into the dimension you experience as "the world."

13

WOUNDS AND HOW THEY SERVE

The wounding becomes sacred when we are willing to release our old stories and become the vehicle through which the new story may emerge into time.

–Jean Houston, *The Search for the Beloved*

As we continue to move deeper into the mystery of relationship, we will eventually have to confront the wounds we carry in our psyche. Traditional psychotherapy treats these wounds as demons to be exorcized. Some religious points of view regard these wounds as "karma" or as "crosses to bear." People who carry their wounds on their sleeves arouse our pity and stir our desire to reach out and attempt to heal those wounds. But what if our wounds are actually our greatest friends? What if our wounds are the catalysts and the energizers that propel us forward on our path, toward the fulfillment of our destiny?

We all carry wounds. Although the circumstances for each of us are unique, we have all been wounded. Not everything has been as we would have wished it to be. We have been hurt. You would probably not be reading this book if you had lived a wound-free life. You would not have been drawn into self-discovery if you were not seeking healing on some level of your Beingness.

Our wounds serve us by giving us the opportunity to develop resources we need in order to fulfill our destiny. What? That's right, our wounds serve. Usually they serve us as individuals, although the way they do so may not fit the preferences of our outer mind. But whether or not a wound appears to serve us as individuals, our wounds do serve Life. Often our wounds allow us to develop the resources to make a unique contribution to the whole. Sometimes the individual is sacrificed and Life is served at the cost of the individual. The tormented artist who contributes a masterwork to the collective is one example of this.

Each wound we carry gives us the opportunity to develop in ways we would not have developed without it—and that serves. Specific wounds offer the opportunity to develop specific resources. In fact, at some level of our totality, our psyche creates exactly the wounds we require in order to develop the specific resources which allow us to contribute to Life whatever we are destined to contribute.

We are not advocating suffering. We are simply observing that, as Brugh Joy points out, crisis creates consciousness. Most of the great contributors to humanity of whom we are aware—the artists, scientists, poets, philosophers, and political leaders—did not grow up in perfect little Ozzie-and-Harriet families. Those who make the greatest contributions to life tend to develop their gifts in the face of, or in response to, their particular wounding.

Sometimes our wounds may not serve us personally, but they do always serve Life. Life does not care about our preferences. We would prefer to be pain-free. We would prefer to be comfortable. Life doesn't care. Life lives us. And Life will develop within the collective the resources needed to serve the collective. Sometimes we are a sacrifice to others, to the collective, to Life. Ken Wilber, a leading transpersonal theorist who has contributed enormously to the awakening of consciousness through his many published works, wrote the book *Grace and Grit*, which tells of the death by cancer of his wife. This story has touched many hearts, and his sharing of their journey through the valley of the shadow of death has made a contribution to Life. It could be argued that his book redeemed his wife's suffering and offered it as a sacrifice for the collective.

Many people have been sacrificed to the evolution of consciousness of the human collective. Many more will be. Many of our most famous people are actually sacrifices to the collective. We are not only speaking of luminaries like Martin Luther King, Jr., and John F. Kennedy, whose deaths represent a sacrifice, but also of people whose circumstances require the sacrifice of privacy and their personal life, as in the cases of such celebrated persons as Princess Diana and Bill Clinton. Have you have ever been among the thousands of fans at a rock concert? If so, you know that regardless of whatever rewards of fame or fortune the rock stars receive, there is also a price to pay. They must sacrifice something of their personal selves to play the role they are playing for the collective.

In most cases, our wounds serve us as individuals even while they scar us. During the years when I—Gawain—was a child, my father had an explosive temper. He often beat me. As a result, I learned to determine my father's moods by reading his facial expressions and body language. I could tell his state of mind around three corners, and I knew when I needed to disappear and when it was safe to stick around. This gave me a heightened sensitivity to other people's states of consciousness and an ability to read energy and body language—qualities that now serve me well as a seminar leader. In the section on patterns and shadows, I will say more about that.

I—Rhea—lived alone with my mother and grandmother in my early childhood. Neither father, brothers, sisters, nor extended family of any kind were available to me. My grandmother worked full-time and my mother worked part-time. It was an emotionally difficult time for my mother and her moods were very unpredictable. In my memory—which means, in the reality of some of my child aspects—she would be loving and fun one moment, screaming and slapping me in the face the next moment, and perhaps sad and tearful the moment after that. I could never be sure how she was going to be.

In looking back, I see that I felt I had to take care of her. I also felt very alone. To handle this I went inside, where my best friend was an "angel." I had several imaginary friends and created inner worlds—worlds in which I was not alone. Through the wound of isolation, I prepared myself to feel at home in the transpersonal realms of consciousness, into which I am now able to guide others.

Also, my experience that I had to, or wanted to, save, protect, and/or take care of my mother was later extended to my wanting to take care of others. Of course, this has its dangers, and much has been written about the so-called negative side of such patterning and the need to develop the ability to take care of oneself and not focus only on taking care of others. However, this "caretaker" pattern has supported me in becoming a therapist and a seminar leader. It has supported me in fulfilling what I perceive to be my destiny.

As an aside, I should mention that the inner children's memory of how a parent was may bear no resemblance to the parent's reality. How parents experience themselves is usually very different from how children experience them. Also, siblings do not have the same parents. I—Rhea—was recently sitting with my two children, listening to them discuss the mother they remember having when they were young. My son obviously had a very different mother than my daughter did, though they are only nineteen months apart in age. They each perceived me through their own projections. I was also clearly aware that "I" was neither of the mothers they were discussing, but was a third entity entirely.

My brother was hit by a car while riding his bicycle when he was nineteen. His head went through the windshield and his brain was injured. He spent a courageous year and a half relearning to walk, talk, and read. After his injury, he went back to school and now holds a master's degree in rehabilitation counseling and is the director of a premier, community re-entry rehabilitation program in Illinois for people with brain injuries.

My son suffered third-degree burns on his leg when he was eleven and required three skin-graft operations. He is now an M.D., in a residency to become a surgeon, and he intends to specialize in reconstructive surgery. No doubt you could add your own examples to those above. Ex-alcoholics counsel others in getting off the bottle. Ex-drug addicts support others in going straight. Our wounds serve Life, through us.

Sometimes, in a seminar, when we are working with people on their purpose in life or attempting to support them in discovering their purpose in life, we will look at their wounds to see what hints we can gather about their destiny. Perhaps you would like to look at your own life as you read the following questions:

What are your wounds?

What happened in your life that you consider hurt you the most?

What resources did having that happen allow you to develop?

What skills or characteristics do you now have that you would not have developed if that set of circumstances had not occurred in your life?

In what area of expression would those resources be most useful?

In what specific job or role in society would the skills that developed from your wounds be most appropriate?

As a result of answering the above questions, many people find that the key to their destiny lies in their wounds.

If you are a parent, you know that one of the most difficult experiences you can have is watching your children be wounded by life. No one on the path of awakening, no parent who is attempting to be conscious, would intentionally wound his or her child. However, no matter how perfect a childhood you have tried to give your children, Life comes along and they get hurt. If the parents do not provide wounds for their children, Life will!

For example, one of our friends who tries to lead a conscious life—we'll call her "Joan"—was determined that her first child would have as perfect a birth as current awareness and knowledge could provide. Joan did everything right during her pregnancy. She was a vegetarian who neither smoked nor drank alcohol or coffee, and she even gave up chocolate for the duration of the pregnancy. Joan and her husband read all the right books and went to the best childbirth classes they could find. Joan swam daily, had acupressure treatments, and even was, herself, rebirthed so her own birth trauma wouldn't interfere with her child's birth experience. The only glitch during the pregnancy was that one of her psychic friends tuned in to the baby around the seventh month of the pregnancy and transmitted the following message from the unborn child: "My mommy is sick but she doesn't know it." Since Joan was in vigorous, perfect health, no one gave much attention to the message.

As her due-date approached, the new hot tub was surrounded with crystals in preparation for a low-trauma water birth. The midwife, acupressurist, and energy-balancer were lined up for the birth. Gawain and I flew in to be present for the event.

119

Nothing happened. After a few days, we had to leave. Time passed. The midwife became concerned. Finally, several days late, Joan went into labor. She spent thirty courageous and determined hours in labor in the hot tub. The baby didn't come. The midwife finally insisted that she go to the hospital. There went the perfect water birth.

After another ten hours of labor in the hospital, the doctors suggested a cesarean. Joan refused, determined at least to have a natural birth for her child.

Although the head was in the birth canal, the baby didn't seem to do any work to be born and no progress was made. After another ten hours of labor, when Joan began to run a fever and the baby was now in danger, the doctors insisted on doing a cesarean and Joan agreed. During the surgery the doctors discovered a tumor the size of a grapefruit on one of Joan's ovaries. The tumor was easily removed and tested benign. The baby was fine after its fifty-hour ordeal and, thanks to her excellent physical condition, Joan recovered relatively quickly. But had the tumor remained undetected, it might have continued to grow and could have become a serious health hazard.

What happened? Life, in its wisdom, intervened and set aside all of Joan's good ideas. The intention to spare the child the wounding of a traumatic birth was overruled by Life. What patterns were activated in the child as a result of the long and difficult birth experience? That remains to be seen. However, what one can be sure of is that the experience shared by Joan and her baby was created by some deeper, inner forces which bypassed the preferences of her outer mind and thereby set the stage for other developments, which may occur many years down the line.

Such things happen to all of us. We may feel frustrated that life did not go the way we preferred, only to discover later that, indeed, Life had a better idea. Can't you look back at a job or relationship you were loathe to let go of, only to find it was replaced by a job or relationship that served you even more than the one you released? Hasn't hindsight shown you that what may have looked like a disaster in the moment actually turned out to be perfect for your development in the long run? We stand there clinging to our daisy and Life is waiting around the corner ready to hand us a bouquet of roses.

With this in mind, we note that a shift in consciousness is available when you begin to regard your wounds as allies instead of enemies. Thus, while some of the examples above make points that are fairly obvious, we'd also like to focus for a moment on something that may not be obvious: the way in which your wounds serve to set the stage for transformation.

Transformation requires energy. What many people never realize, however, is that through the wound the individual is given energy. This energy sets into motion a certain sequence of events that would not have occurred without the wound. Then, later in life, you will encounter an opportunity to redeem the wound. This means you will have the chance to recognize how the wound served you and to consciously embrace the resources the wound allowed you to develop. This conscious act of recognizing how the wound served you—how you would not be who you are without that wound—leads to a transformation of consciousness that redeems the wound. Through this process you become bigger. Your experience of your totality is expanded. The wound has then fulfilled its purpose. Redeeming your wounds requires feeling the pain still held in them. To wake up to the fullness of your Being, to claim your wholeness, you will have to undergo that conscious suffering.

We are not saying that everyone will consciously redeem the wounds they have unconsciously created for themselves. Many people will never move beyond the victim/victimizer point of view. However, even if people don't consciously redeem their wounds, they nevertheless serve Life by having gone through the process of being wounded. People who become healers due to an unconscious desire to heal their own pain may never consciously realize why they were motivated to become healers, yet they still serve Life by healing others.

Any deep, intimate, relationship will reactivate your wounds. When you learn how to appreciate those wounds, acknowledging what they cost you but also appreciating how they contributed to your life, then you can use the reactivation that is triggered in your relationship as a way to become more aware. You can begin to recognize that your partner is serving you, assisting you to become more conscious, because any part of your totality you have not yet claimed, any suppressed emotion or incomplete experience, will eventually surface in your relationship.

As you open to the love between you and your partner, you must also open to your own pain. You cannot open to one emotion without opening to all emotions. Likewise you cannot shut down one emotion without shutting down your ability to experience all emotions. You can't say: "I'll take the love but not the pain." By and by, you also realize that whatever pain your partner appears to be causing you actually has nothing to do with your partner. He or she may trigger the pain, but it is yours and it was in you before that other person ever came along. Once you see that, you are ready to begin opening to your own shadow material.

14

PATTERNS AND SHADOWS

Everyone carries a shadow, and the less it is embodied in the individual's conscious life, the blacker and denser it is.

—C. G. Jung

We have already discussed shadow material in the section on projection. As we indicated in that chapter, in this book we use the term "shadow" to indicate those parts of our psyche of which we are unconscious—those parts of ourselves we do not see. Many of our life decisions and interactions flow out of this shadow material, though we are usually totally unconscious of that fact. We should remember that the shadow is not negative; it is simply that which is unseen. In this section we will take a close look at how the shadow parts of our psyche can show up in relationship.

We have come to recognize that bringing shadow material into consciousness creates suffering. Even if what is uncovered is actually quite wonderful, shifting one's self-image is painful. In some ways, it is just as difficult for those who have always considered themselves worthless to discover they have wonderful qualities as it is for those who have always thought they were "good" to discover parts of themselves that are not so flattering. The ego, or personality structure, has a difficult time when we discover that we are not who we thought we were. We become attached to our perception of ourselves—for good or ill—and letting go of that perception is not easy.

Confronting parts of yourself you have actually spent a great deal of energy attempting to avoid is hard. Your image of who you are is wounded when you begin to recognize parts of your totality you didn't know were there. However, you have to suffer these realizations about yourself if you are committed to moving toward wholeness. As seminar leaders, for example, we know that if we attempt to protect people in our groups from these realizations about themselves, seeking to spare them the suffering of seeing parts of themselves they didn't know were there, we rob them of an opportunity to gain consciousness. Through the suffering involved in recognizing and eventually embracing their shadow, they gain consciousness.

There are many ways to begin to recognize your shadow. One is through your dreams. Another, as we discussed earlier, is by looking at who or what upsets you in your outer reality. What types of movies do you avoid? What particular crime or event disturbs you the most when you read the newspaper? What kind of behavior most offends you?

You can get a clue about your own shadow material by looking at someone you simply cannot stand. What qualities does he or she carry that most disturb you? That's right—somewhere, those qualities exist in you. Ouch! What about the opposite sex? What type of person of the opposite sex would you least like to be stuck in a broken elevator with? Ouch again! You can also look at your parents and see what about each of them you really dislike—then look for those qualities or a variation of those qualities in yourself.

In relationship, your partner will dramatize your unconscious material for you, and knowing that happens is useful. Whatever you don't like about your partner, whatever upsets you about your partner is, in the end, a characteristic of your own being that you have not yet owned. If you use your relationship as a way to recognize your own shadow material, you wrestle a bit of darkness into the light—you are coming into greater consciousness.

In this section we will share with you some of the patterns and shadows we have discovered in ourselves. We do so in the hope that you may recognize something about yourself as you read. We have consciously chosen to present some of our more difficult moments. We aren't talking here about the many good times we've had together, because when you're having good times, difficulties don't usually come up. And right now, we're talking about the times when things do come up. When the shit hits the fan, knowing a way out of the situation becomes important. For this purpose, we

124

share a few of our difficulties and what we discovered about ourselves along the way.

Though the issues and tensions that surface in your relationship may be different from those we share in the following pages, the principle for solving them is the same. What finally serves your development is the willingness to be vulnerable and open, to take a look at what lies under an upset—even though being willing to be vulnerable might not be your immediate response. But if you are willing to look and take responsibility for what you discover under the tension or the upset, your relationship and your self-awareness will both benefit.

So, as you read about us, we invite you to look at yourself. The name at the beginning of each section indicates who is speaking.

Gawain

I love windsurfing. During the last five years, I have spent many hours practicing the skills one needs to be proficient at this sport. Windsurfing is very difficult, because it combines the need for physical strength, a sense of balance, and an ability to coordinate many variables simultaneously— variables such as wind direction and velocity, water and wave conditions, sail angle, and the presence of other surfers. It also requires the willingness to go out onto the ocean and to handle one's fear of the natural elements. Since I love this sport so much, Rhea has also become involved in windsurfing and has tried to master the necessary skills. I have fully supported her in those efforts.

In July 1992, we returned for our regular vacation to Fuerteventura, one of the Canary Islands and a prime windsurfing location. The apartment where we stayed has a beautiful, rock-free, sandy beach. At low tide, I can walk out into the water for more than a hundred meters without going deeper than my waist. The ocean there can also be dangerous, since the winds are offshore (meaning that they blow out to sea—next stop Africa). In July and August, winds average twenty to forty-plus miles per hour. Every year, one or two windsurfers have an equipment breakdown and get blown out to sea because no one sees them. When nobody sees them and comes to their aid, they are lost. Rhea learned to windsurf in that challenging environment.

In order to provide background for the story I am about to relate, I have to mention an incident that occurred in the same location two years earlier.

At that time, Rhea was starting to get more comfortable with the sport, even though she was afraid of going out into deep water. With my encouragement, she pushed her limits and went farther out into the ocean than she had before. Suddenly, as the wind got stronger, she fell into the water. Her attempts to restart and return to shore failed, since she didn't have the physical strength, given the sudden increase in wind strength, to lift the sail out of the water.

In this sport, as a beginner, you start by standing on the board and pulling the sail—which has been lying flat on the water's surface—out of the water with a thick nylon rope. As the sail clears the water you grab a horizontal boom that is attached to the mast and hold the sail into the wind, balancing the wind pressure with your body weight. As you pull the sail up from the water's surface, the wind has already begun to fill the portion of it that is in the air, thereby creating pressure which you have to balance through your own body strength. The stronger the wind, the greater the pressure you must counteract. As Rhea tried to start sailing back to shore in this fashion, she didn't have enough strength to pull the sail up out of the water without having it blown out of her hands. The wind had become too strong. As I saw what was happening to her, I sailed out to her with my own board and tried to help her back to shore, but was unsuccessful.

We were very fortunate that our neighbors, who lived in the apartment next to ours, had been watching what was going on with us through binoculars and sent someone to a local hotel to request that they dispatch a boat to rescue us. When we were finally safe, we had been adrift on the ocean for more than two hours.

Naturally, after that, Rhea was very careful how far she went out when she was surfing. She was always worried that the wind would suddenly pick up and she would be unable to get back to shore.

The incident made me aware of how unconscious I was about other people's limits. I am an expert swimmer. I am very good at handling my body, and I have practiced sports all my life. I had no idea of what these difficult windsurfing conditions were like for someone who was afraid of deep water and whose body was not as agile as mine. My encouraging her to go out into deep water was not very intelligent. She floated out into the ocean because *I wanted her to master windsurfing*. At the time, I didn't know why I was willing to risk her getting into such a dangerous situation just so she would learn to surf. However, I did notice that I really push *myself* to become better and better at windsurfing. I recognized that I compared myself incessantly to other windsurfers, those I thought were better than I was.

That was the prelude. Here is the story.

Rhea was out practicing her windsurfing skills, working on a difficult maneuver called a waterstart. During a waterstart the surfer is not standing on the board pulling the sail out of the water but is in the water next to the board, holding the sail at a precise angle to the wind so the force of the wind against the sail lifts the surfer onto the board. Once this can be done, he or she no longer has to pull the sail out of the water, which is a big advantage in strong winds. Actually, standing on the board and pulling the sail up out of the water is almost impossible in high winds. That, in fact, was how Rhea got in trouble earlier, when the winds arose and she could no longer pull up the sail. If she had been able to do a waterstart, she would not have drifted out to sea.

As she practiced this new skill I noticed that I was very impatient with her. I criticized her constantly, and even if she did something well, I still pointed out what wasn't working. I justified my critical coaching with the notion that one can always improve and that such improvement is the only way to really achieve superior skills. Obviously, however, being constantly criticized was not much fun for Rhea, and she told me so.

As she continued to practice her windsurfing maneuvers, I saw that she was avoiding going out very far into the ocean. I realized this was probably because she was still being careful not to be blown out to sea again.

That really made me angry. When she came back to shore, I said to her, "How can you expect to learn anything, especially planing, if you don't surf out far enough so you *can* plane?" (Planing is windsurfing very fast; it is the addictive part of the sport.) As I said this, I was angry and irritated, and I communicated my feelings by my facial expressions, tone of voice, and body language.

Rhea said, "It isn't much fun when you always tell me what I'm doing wrong."

Hesitantly, I agreed, and she went out again to practice. This time she even had difficulty getting up on the board. Finally, she managed to do it, but after going only a short distance, tried to turn around and come back in.

I was furious. Again she didn't go out far enough. I was disgusted. I turned around and went back to our apartment, alone. "Why can't she listen to me?" I was thinking as I stalked off. "She'll never learn how to surf."

After a while, Rhea finished practicing and came back to the apartment. "Where were you?" she asked.

"I came back in," I replied.

"I saw that," she said. "What happened?"

I got angry and told her she would never be able to windsurf if she didn't conquer her fear of going out into deep water. She responded sarcastically, again saying something about how much fun she was having.

So I said, "What do you mean?"

She responded by shrugging her shoulders. (You know the drill. Surely you have been there a time or two.)

Then I got really angry, and I asked her again, "What do you mean? You think I don't want you to have fun? Windsurfing *is* fun, but first you have to suffer through the learning stage. We all have to do it."

Then, of course, she told me I didn't understand her, and the fight continued.

After a while we began to communicate. We decided we would both do what we call "outflowing"—a communication session. One of us would listen while the other talked, then we would switch roles.

After the communication session, we did indeed feel clearer. The upset was gone and we had each shifted into more mature aspects of our inner communities—aspects that were aware of how much we love each other. The issue hadn't exactly dissolved but we felt better. We agreed that my agitation had to do with my desire to have her as a skilled windsurfing partner who could share this experience with me.

The next day, the last day before we would fly home from our vacation, the same pattern started to unfold. The wind was not very strong and it was ideal for Rhea's intermediate skill-level. She went out, but only a short distance, then she turned around. Again I felt the irritation that bordered on anger that she wouldn't even use these perfect conditions, this ideal set-up, to practice properly.

Suddenly, I remembered my father. He often got upset with me. No matter how hard I tried, I could never do anything right for him. Suddenly I realized: *I am acting just like my father*. I was repeating his behavior exactly. I was showing the same impatience and irritability with Rhea that he had showed with me. I was shocked. Then I heard the word "failure" floating around in my head and I got it. I cannot bear to experience failure, in myself or in the people around me. Failure means pain. Failure means I haven't done it right. Failure means punishment from my father, both emotionally and physically.

In that moment, I both realized and experienced that I was still acting out an old drama that started around 1963, when, at the age of ten, I first assisted my father in his job. The frightened ten-year-old boy in my inner community was dominating the whole windsurfing drama with Rhea . . . thirty years later. In my ten-year-old's mentality, failure has to be avoided at all costs. Failure must also be avoided in anything or anyone I identify with. Since, at times, I do identify with Rhea, she became part of this internal drama. I also suddenly realized that my drive to master many skills, and my continual dissatisfaction with what I have achieved, was fueled by my fear of failure.

After that insight, as I looked at Rhea surfing toward the shore, I realized that all of my impatience, irritation, and anger had disappeared. Suddenly what she was doing looked beautiful, almost heroic, given her disposition with regard to athletic pursuits. Suddenly I could see how much she had achieved. She has never participated much in sports, yet she had managed to learn to windsurf under very difficult conditions. Absolutely fantastic!

My perception of reality changed when I recognized which aspect of my inner community had been in charge of my psyche (the frightened child) and what pattern was in charge of that aspect (avoid pain by avoiding failure). Rhea looked totally different to me now than she had a very short time before. Truly, outer reality is transformed as we wake up to the filters through which we perceive ourselves and others.

As this realization sank in, what I was left with was—pain. I could finally experience all the emotional pain of the ten-year-old boy who frantically tried to do everything right to avoid the wrath of his father. I let myself feel the pain. I realized that even the resignation I felt with Rhea when I was disgusted with her progress was a repeat of something I had experienced with my father. When I failed for a time in school, he gave up on me, ignoring me for years, since I did not fulfill his expectations. That was painful. Again, I was shocked as I recognized how much I display my father's patterning, *even though I had vowed as an adolescent never to be like him.* I had unconsciously projected that entire drama from my childhood onto this windsurfing incident in my present life with Rhea.

This pattern was totally shadow material. Although, looking back, I could see that the pattern often dominated my life, I had never been consciously aware of it. If someone had asked me if I was afraid of failure, I would have responded, "Of course not." Through this incident, however, a whole new part of my psyche and its patterning became available to my conscious awareness. I saw the source of my competitiveness and my urge always to become better at whatever I am doing. Because of that drive, incidentally, I could never enjoy what I had achieved for very long. In the end, nothing was ever enough.

Although, as I write this, I am still in the process of experiencing the old pain, I also understand that this patterning served me. I would never have developed my various skills had I not been pushed from within by my strong fear of failing. That fear of failing is what pushed me into doing everything I could do to be perfect, in everything in which I became involved. Unfortunately, as I learned, when one is dominated by such a pattern one can never enjoy the fruit of one's labor. Having now recognized this basic pattern of mine, I feel that in the future I will be able to relax much more with myself and my surroundings, and so be really able to enjoy the skills I have developed.

Once you have identified a pattern and felt it emotionally, recognizing and handling that pattern will be much easier when it resurfaces—and it surely will. The moment you are aware of the appearance of a recurring pattern, its energy collapses into a big, "Ah-ha, here I go again." The awareness of how much of your behavior is run by these patterns is very humbling . . . until you forget and life reminds you again, and again.

Rhea

One of my favorite quotes is from a sixteenth-century Spanish poet named Calderon de la Barca. He said: "La vida es sueno y los suenos, suenos son." (Life is a dream and dreams are dreams, also.) The quote reminds me that the events of one's life can be read as if they were a dream. Doing so offers another way to gain insight into one's unconscious, or shadow, material.

In the preceding section, Gawain described an experience we had when I was windsurfing, could not get back to shore, and began drifting out into the ocean. This occurred at a time in my life when I was consciously working with opening to what I perceive to be the feminine aspects of the psyche. That is to say, I was consciously attempting to surrender to life rather than to shape life. In my seminar work, the presence of the Great Mother and of her counterpart, Kali, had begun to come forward when I entered an expanded state of consciousness. These energies were very strong, and while the participants in the groups obviously found value in being exposed to them, I personally was having a difficult time trusting and letting go of control so those forces could come forward. My own masculine aspects wanted to conceptualize and control what was happening spontaneously and those parts of myself had a hard time trusting that everything was okay.

When I began to look at that incident of drifting out to sea from the viewpoint of its being a dream, which I could interpret as I would interpret any dream, I had a deep insight into my internal process. When Gawain and I work with a dream, we assume that everyone in the dream represents an aspect of the dreamer. Thus, in the "dream," I am encouraged by Gawain (one of my masculine aspects) to venture out into the ocean (the unconscious, the transpersonal). I wanted to go and I did go. However, I went out into the ocean farther than I should have, given the level of my skills. I was literally in over my head! I did not have the resources to deal with the forces (of the unconscious). Nor were my own male aspects (symbolized by Gawain) able to save me, though they tried. I kept drifting farther away from shore, farther from solid ground. I thought I was going to die. I was terrified.

However, though we didn't know it at the time, our neighbors were watching us and sent for help. Because of them, I was rescued and brought back to shore. While looking at the entire scene as a "dream," I interpreted our neighbors as being forces that are watching over me, though I may not be aware of such forces. The dream indicates that I am protected by an unseen resource that will bring me back to shore—to solid ground—even if I do overestimate my ability to venture into the transpersonal ranges of consciousness.

The shadow content revealed by the dream/event was that I am, indeed, capable of doing just that: overestimating my skills when dealing with the transpersonal. It was a warning to respect the power of those forces. So the message I got was: I can venture into the new arenas of the transpersonal feminine that were spontaneously coming forward in the groups, because I was protected. At the same time it was a strong warning to develop my skills and to respect the power of the vast feminine ranges of experience.

A year later we returned to Fuerteventura for what had become our annual, one-month retreat. One evening, I suddenly felt drawn to go for a walk. I "happened" to walk to the beach where the above event had taken place the year before. The time of day was the same—the sun was just beginning to set. I thought the area was deserted. Then I saw a man, silhouetted by the setting sun, standing on a low hill just off the beach. He seemed to be staring at the beach. As I walked onto the sand, I saw what he was looking at. A form was lying near the water. I approached. It was a dead man. His body was purple and bloated and he had obviously drowned. Someone had carefully placed a pair of black rubber swim fins on his chest. In the fading light it was a macabre sight and I was shaken to my core.

I walked over to the man on the hill and asked him (in halting German, since that beach was mostly used by German tourists) if he knew what had happened. He said he was a friend of the drowned man. He had pulled him out of the water and sent for the police. He said there was nothing I could do. In what now seems to me to be a bizarre expression of my desire to do *something* (and an unfortunate reflection of my perception of Germans), I asked him if I could get him a beer. His grimace was almost a smile as he refused.

As I left the beach, I stopped for a moment and tried to connect with the spirit of the drowned man and, holding an image of a column of white light, attempted to soothe his frightened spirit and encourage it to leave this dimension. Having done all I thought I could, I went back to our apartment and told Gawain. He wanted to see the body, so he returned alone to the beach. I was still shaken and didn't want to go back, so I lay down.

Though I had left the scene only five minutes earlier, the beach was empty when Gawain got there. The body had been removed in the short time it took him to return and all evidence that the event ever took place was gone. When Gawain came back, he questioned me about what had happened and I had to assure him that I had actually seen the body. Obviously the event was not for Gawain, as I was the one who had been drawn to the beach to witness it. It was my "dream."

Since I had already worked on the events of the year before as a dream—as a gift from my unconscious, which was attempting to communicate something to me through the symbols of so-called outer reality—I realized that this was the sequel to that earlier dream/event. (Again, time means nothing to the unconscious. That a year had passed was inconsequential. I knew a connection existed.) This part of the dream/event told me that, indeed, one of my masculine aspects had not survived the forces of the unconscious. I saw the dead man as a substitution sacrifice for myself—in a way, because he died, "I" didn't have to, though a part of me clearly had.

This sequel affirmed my experience in our seminars, which was that as I continued to open consciously to the forces of the transpersonal aspects of the feminine, some aspect of my own inner masculine had "died." As I relaxed and allowed a new part of myself, a more essentially feminine part, to come forward, I had to let go of a portion of myself and shift my experience of who I perceived myself to be.

When you begin to look at the events in your life as if they are a dream, you have another tool for bringing the material and/or the dynamics of your unconscious to consciousness. If you want to try this for yourself, just write out the events of one of the strong experiences in your life. Then read what you have written as if you were reading someone else's dream. This will give you a little distance from the experience and perhaps make it easier to see the symbols and patterns. "La vida es sueno . . . . "

Gawain

Earlier in this book I mentioned a time when I thought Rhea was insecure, only to discover that I had been projecting onto her my own feeling of insecurity. Here's what happened.

In our seminars, we often use an active meditation called the Five-Rhythm Meditation (it is described fully in "Riding Lessons"). The meditation makes use of the qualities associated with the five basic body rhythms, which are: 1) round/flowing, 2) staccato, 3) chaotic, 4) lyrical, and 5) stillness. From working with this meditation, I have come to see that these basic movements can also be observed in different types of people. For example, we all know people whose basic expression is round and flowing, others who function in a staccato rhythm, and still others who are chaotic types, and so on. A large part of my own psyche operates in staccato energy, while Rhea is more the round-and-flowing type.

When Rhea and I are leading a seminar, at times we do what we call "circle work." We sit on the floor in a circle with the other people while they ask questions or share experiences and we respond. Rhea usually takes her time in responding. Sometimes people in the seminar even think she has forgotten about them. My responses, by contrast, are usually very quick.

Well, in the early years of our working together, during this circle work, I used to get irritated with Rhea when her answers were slow in coming or when she showed any hesitation. My irritation was even greater when she appeared to be unsure in her response. If that happened, I would whisper to her, "What is going on, Rhea? People are waiting. What's happening?"

For me to experience any hesitation or slowness in her reactions was excruciating. I began to believe she was insecure. During the break, I would talk to her and ask her why she was so insecure. I wanted to know what was going on with her. She, however, usually felt fine with her reactions and wondered why I was so agitated. I said that her insecurity was very clear and obvious and that I was embarrassed for her in front of the group. These feelings came up for me from time to time for years.

Then one day, as we were leading a seminar, the same thing happened. I was about to plug into my usual reaction when suddenly I became *aware*. I abruptly realized that *I* was the one who was insecure, not Rhea. That was a shock. In that moment, I felt the experience of insecurity filling my whole body. After the session ended, I told Rhea of my revelation. She smiled and said she had known it all along, but I was never able to hear it from her.

This is an example of a shadow aspect of consciousness. I was completely unaware of my insecurity and that I had actually projected it onto Rhea. By blaming her for it, however, I could avoid feeling insecure myself. Especially since I considered insecurity a weakness in others, avoided people who displayed it, and judged them negatively for it, I—by blaming Rhea for being insecure—actually expressed an unconscious judgment of myself.

The presence of this unconscious insecurity ties in to my fear of being a failure, which I discussed earlier. My unconscious strategy was that by accusing Rhea and asking her to change her behavior (to answer the

134

questions faster), I hoped to avoid experiencing the embarrassing gap of silence and feeling the possibility that I was somehow implicated in her "failure." In that way, I hoped to get out of the situation that triggered my own sense of insecurity.

This is another example of projection and the illusions it creates. My attitude toward Rhea and my ideas about her and the situation were a complete illusion. What I had thought was absolutely true turned out to be not the case—*totally* not the case. What I accused Rhea of was actually what I carried within myself. All of my behavior in these situations was just an unconscious strategy to avoid the experience of feeling insecure.

When I looked at this pattern, I saw that all of my life I had been attracted to powerful people who were sure of themselves. I wanted to be around people who did not display any insecurity at all, and in that way I hoped to protect myself from the possibility of experiencing my own insecurity. Of course, I tried to become just like my models. All of my gurus and teachers, therefore, had to be infallible. They had to demonstrate that they were completely in control of life. In the spiritual arena, where the surrender of control is usually regarded as a virtue, I found myself admiring an allow-everything-to-happen-the-way-it-wants-to-happen-and-then-there-is-bliss attitude. What this attitude *actually* implied to me was that by consciously abdicating any control whatsoever, I was, in fact, experiencing another, superior type of control. In effect the attitude said, "I'm in control of the fact that I'm not in control."

When one of my heroes failed, I abandoned that person and looked for another. If I were to acknowledge that a hero had failed, yet still allow him or her to be my hero, that would mean my own inner feeling of insecurity and fear of failing would be available for me to experience. Of course, at some level, I knew this fear and insecurity were present within me, but I was unconsciously trying to avoid experiencing the pain connected with it. It was too threatening. Holding to the ideal of possible perfection and simply looking for another hero to fill that image was easier.

If you look at people's heroes, you can tell a lot about their inadequacies and hidden fears. The heroes will carry the qualities the people feel they, themselves, lack. The heroes compensate for those areas where people feel they fall short.

My search for a "perfect" teacher was a compensation for my lack of peace with regard to my own self-perceived imperfection. The revelation about my insecurity allowed me to see a lot about myself, my attitudes toward life, and my choices in life. In this process, Rhea served me by playing out the part she did and by staying in communication with me, even as I falsely accused her.

This is also another example of how a committed relationship can serve a person in becoming aware. Before I was in a committed relationship with Rhea, I always avoided situations where real or imagined weakness might be present. But through being in our relationship, I woke up to the presence of what was actually shadow material within my own psyche. Again, we must be aware of who and what we point our finger at. Our judgments of others invariably say more about ourselves than they do about who or what we are judging.

Rhea

Gawain and I had a fight. We were driving back to our home in southern Germany from a weekend seminar we had led in Zurich. We were discussing the seminar and Gawain started talking about something he didn't like— something I said to one of the participants. He thought I had been reactivated by her because she disagreed with me. He went on to observe that I just can't stand to be disagreed with.

That did it! I was not centered. I was not even considering the possibility of whether I was in a child aspect or in a mature aspect of consciousness. I was angry. I responded: "What do you mean, I have a hard time being disagreed with? Why do you always have to put me down and tell me what's wrong with me?" The fight was on!

Under my anger, of course, was pain. What he had said really hurt my feelings. I felt devastated. But when I looked at why I was so hurt by what Gawain had said, I couldn't figure it out. What he said seemed to be the source of my pain, but I knew the pain was out of proportion to what apparently provoked it. His words, which I took as a put-down, did not warrant my feeling the amount of pain I felt.

I looked deeper and asked myself where all the pain was coming from. I was amazed. What I found was guilt at how much I had judged my mother and made her wrong. As a teenager, I had been merciless in my judgments of her. For the most part, my judgments had been silent. But I had allowed my righteous contempt to show just enough so she knew she had no chance with me. It was difficult to confront the way I had treated her.

Looking back, I could justify that scorn as a necessary stage in my own individuation process. However, the pain of what I had done to this person I loved above all others was almost overwhelming. I now could see that the righteousness I felt when anything negative was directed toward me was a way of protecting myself from that pain. I unconsciously felt guilty about how hard I had been on my mother when I was growing up. So when others made unflattering judgments about me, I projected that guilt onto them and made them wrong. That is, I used *them* to make myself wrong. Judging them for their negative judgments was my way of unconsciously judging myself for what I had done to my mother. My unconscious guilt was also probably related to why I sometimes manipulated Gawain into punishing me by saying negative things about me.

Before I discuss the next incident, I'd like to lay a little groundwork. Perhaps this sounds a bit off-the-wall, but my observation is that somewhere in most of us, in our inner community, is an aspect that does not want to be here. Doesn't want to be on Earth in a body and resents the fact that it is stuck here. That aspect seems to think a mistake was made by the cosmic bureaucracy and, through some accident, it got sent by the bureaucracy to the wrong dimension. Or, its spaceship was really headed for Sirius and had a meltdown and got stranded on this planet. (Sort of a grownup's version of the child who *knows* it must have been adopted—these *can't* be its real parents.) I certainly know I have an aspect that is sure its having turned up in a body on Earth was a mistake!

This incident happened just after we had led a weekend workshop in Utah. It was our first seminar in the States for a couple of years. I was happy to do some work in America because, although I love working in Europe, as an American I often miss being "home." Earlier in the day, I told a friend on the phone that I felt like a volcano waiting to explode. Within hours of my saying that, my entire face broke out in a painful rash for no apparent reason. After the seminar, on the drive back to Santa Fe, Gawain and I started fighting. I was very angry. Again, I noticed that my emotion was out of proportion to the circumstances that appeared to be the source of the upset. I looked deeper.

I have trained myself to work with my emotions when they seem out of proportion to what is happening in my life at the moment, but I still didn't recognize that my anger, the energy of that inner volcano, was not really directed at Gawain. It took me some moments of trying to center to see that the anger at Gawain was just a way to vent an emotion that lay much deeper. *I was really angry at God.* The aspect of my consciousness that was in charge at the moment felt that if I got my job done, then God would win. Doing "the work" (which I see as supporting people in remembering or recognizing who they really are) on American soil somehow seemed like getting my job done. And if I got my job done, "HE" would have been right to have sent me here (to Earth, in a body), which was *not* all right with me. I didn't want "HIM" to win. If I got my job done (somehow leading seminars abroad didn't count in the moment, like shopping with foreign money doesn't count) then it was as if I was saying that all of the pain of being human was okay. My right to protest getting "stuck" on Earth would have been negated.

The aspect of my inner community that doesn't want to be here definitely had the microphone. It was in charge of my emotions, as "I" raged against God. Silently, I let myself scream at God—let myself say everything I resented about being human. Sitting with my eyes closed next to Gawain in the car as he drove, I went on and on until nothing was left inside me. Then, after the insight, the breakthrough, and the tears, came the beginning of acceptance and integration of that defiant aspect into my inner community. Gradually I felt myself shift into another aspect, one that accepted and even enjoyed being human.

Until this experience, I had no idea how much pain I had been carrying in the part of me that didn't want to be a human being. I could also begin to appreciate why I had been working in Europe and South America and Australia—anywhere but the States. A lot of pieces began fitting together. I thought about the fact that as soon as I had gone from having a private practice and leading small groups to leading larger groups, I started working in Europe. My first five books had been published in Europe and South America but not in the States (though we published my first book, *A Call to the Lightworkers,* in English ourselves). Now I could see that a part of me had not wanted to work in the U.S. because, given the particular software of my inner computer, that would have been making God "right."

As I look back at those two upsets with Gawain, I can see the incredible service the relationship provided, as it allowed me to break through to levels of inner pain I didn't even know existed. I could see that feeling the pain in the upset with Gawain was a way for me to begin getting to the real pain, which was beneath my conscious awareness and had been trying to surface. But I needed a catalyst of some sort in order to get to it. In fact, I could almost feel part of myself creating the upset so shadow material could come to light.

Of course, the work I had done on myself earlier helped. I was aware, for example, that most current upsets are echoes of earlier incidents, so I knew enough to realize that my anger was out of proportion to what was actually happening and I looked for a deeper, older source of the emotion I was feeling. When one has not learned, or having learned does not remember, to stop in the middle of an argument and ask oneself, "What is really going on here? What is underneath this upset?" and stays instead at the level of the surface upset—one cannot usually get to the underlying distress. Then one must keep creating painful experiences to give oneself a chance to uncover the pain and get free from it by finally fully experiencing it. Fortunately, my partner was also willing to let go of the superficial disagreement when we realized something else was happening—that some deeper mystery was afoot. Gawain provided me with an awesome gift by allowing me to move through this process with him.

Gawain

There is a part of me that has always been attracted to the seedy side of sexuality. And I have a tendency to hide the fact. In the beginning of my relationship with Rhea, I told her about this inclination. I continued sharing about sexual issues with her, including my likes and dislikes, even when doing so was uncomfortable. Still, it took me a while to recognize and communicate that, at times, I avoided having sex with her by masturbating while watching sex films or looking at sex magazines. When I did recognize this avoidance, I realized that the Madonna/whore syndrome was active in my psyche.

As we mentioned in the section on sexuality, the Madonna/whore syndrome is a defense many men employ in order not to confront their incestuous feelings toward their mothers. The man splits "woman" into a dark and a light aspect with regard to sexuality. The dark aspect, the whore, serves as an image for disowned sexual material. Those dark aspects will be different from man to man, depending on his conditioning. They will be those areas of sexuality he could never perceive as being part of his mother's life, and they will be those areas for which he could never imagine getting his mother's approval. The light aspect, the Madonna, serves the aspects in the man that allow him to keep the image of the mother, usually as a nonsexual being, intact. In this way, a man attempts to avoid the dangerous truth that he is/was sexually attracted to his mother, and that any woman (his mother included!) is a complete Being, containing both Madonna and whore aspects. Men who unconsciously try to save their image of their mother as nonsexual express this syndrome. They then will engage in the approved-of version of sex with their wives while hoping to fulfill their more seamy sexual desires outside the marriage—either with another woman or, as I did, with a substitute in the form of videos and magazines.

That is the background—here is the story.

We were in Santa Fe. Rhea was out running an errand. I watched a sex video at home and masturbated while watching it. When Rhea came home I told her about having done so, in line with our agreement not to keep any secrets. As I have said, I discovered early on that acknowledging the truth about my sexual inclinations was hard for me, so I had decided to acknowledge such things to Rhea immediately, as a way of breaking through the shame/hiding cycle. While she is often fine with such information, that day when I told her what had happened, I could immediately see she was upset.

She left the office in our home where I was working and went into the bedroom, leaving me with her apparent rejection. I got upset. Why was she being so pissy about it? I thought she must have some sexual hangups of her own she was not acknowledging. She was always telling me that the whole issue with the sex videos was just about telling the truth. But look at her behavior. Obviously, she must not be aware of some of her own stuff . . . or so went my reasoning.

After a while I got more agitated. What right did she have to spoil my whole day by being pissy? We had been in harmony. Now she was destroying it with her attitude. I went into the bedroom and said, "Come on, Rhea, get off it. I did exactly what we agreed to do. You don't have any right to be upset." When she didn't seem to get off it, I blew up. I told her she wasn't taking responsibility for her reaction and that I had to suffer because of it.

I felt extremely upset. I gathered some things together and walked out. I was oozing righteous indignation. I got in the car and sped off, headed toward Colorado, about one hundred miles north of our home. (We all know that leaving is a way of trying to escape the inner pain—which, of course, is impossible.) When I stopped in southern Colorado to spend the night in a motel, I was still feeling righteous, though I was also feeling the pain that was beginning to seep through my defenses. Alternating with the experience of pain, what kept coming to my mind was the idea of "freedom." I thought, "Why do I have to tell anybody what I am thinking and doing? When I lived alone it was no one's business what I did, and I felt great. Why do I have to tell Rhea anything? I am no longer a free Being. People should be together because they love each other out of free will. There shouldn't be any demands on the other—just a free sharing. People should give each other the room to be who and what they are, without demanding that they be different." A quote from Werner Erhard even came to mind, one I heard back in the early eighties: "Real love is loving your partner just the way he/she is and the way he/she is not." Rhea was definitely not fulfilling that ideal.

The next morning I called her and reluctantly announced my conclusion that sacrificing the relationship over the upset was, perhaps, overreacting. I told her I was coming back.

As I drove into our garage in Santa Fe, Rhea came out to meet me and was very cheerful and open. I was not. I still felt I was morally right and therefore I was closed and tense. After a few hours of continuing to try to blame Rhea (she didn't take the bait but, instead, stayed centered), I suddenly felt my pain. The defense that I had been "wronged" by Rhea began to dissolve.

I have learned that when any of us has the feeling that we are "right" about something in a relationship, it is often a defense to protect us from having to feel our own pain. Since Rhea, rather than resisting my abrasive energy, was staying centered, no one was any longer "playing the ball back into my court," and my deeper feelings rushed up. Rhea, as I perceived her, was suddenly transformed from a righteous bitch into a wonderfully sensitive Being, and I once again was in touch with myself.

We went into the bedroom and I lay down on the bed. I began breathing deeply in order to connect with my feelings, to open to the pain consciously, so I could take a clear look at what was really going on. What came up was astonishing.

I remembered being a little boy, three years old, playing with my penis. My mother found me and gave me a stern admonition: "Don't do that! That's bad." I suddenly felt terrible. My beloved mother had said I was bad! As a little boy I could not distinguish between my actions and myself, so, for the first time in my life, I decided *I* was bad. (Which is to say that a latent pattern in me became activated.) Next came the thought, "I am bad and my mother doesn't love me."

As I—the adult—lay there, breathing into the feelings associated with this early decision, more and more pain surfaced and I found myself sobbing. Mother, the center of my universe, had rejected me! For young children that is a devastating wound. And the children will usually find *in themselves* the reason for the rejection. The children will then make the parent right for rejecting them by blaming themselves. The children feel that the problem is their own fault. The children do not have the awareness to realize that the parents are acting out of their own wounds and attempting to avoid their own pain. For the infant/child, the parent is godlike, and so obviously something must be wrong with the children, not the parents.

Immediately following the "I am bad" decision I made as a child, came the conclusion: "I can never be good." That judgment, which many of us make, is usually accompanied by the decision, "I am a bad person." This decision is then amplified by the feeling that we will never be able to atone for the terrible thing we have done. As a consequence of these decisions, at age three, my next thought was, "I am alone." (Others often make this same decision, too—a fact we have confirmed after hearing the same decision-making sequences reported many times in our seminars.)

Mother is the major point of orientation in the outer universe for a small child. The moment infants or children first recognize rejection from Mother, they experience themselves as separate from her. That experience of separation is painful, an echo of the *big* separation of being expelled from the womb. (This is why any experience of separation from a loved one is difficult for our infantile aspects—it reactivates the feelings of the first separation from Mother.)

As I allowed myself to feel the overwhelming sense of an aloneness I had never permitted myself to experience fully as a child, another layer of pain opened within me. And it drew me into the next major inner decision I made as a child. It was, "I don't belong here. I am lost." (Another latent pattern activated.) As I felt deeply into the emotions connected to these early, previously unconscious decisions, I suddenly saw my entire life in a completely new light. I now recognized that many of my major choices in life had been influenced by this major wound, which I received from my mother as a small child. The decision "I am bad" was simply more than I could handle as a young child.

As I had these insights, lying on the bed in Santa Fe, I could see that I had, after that event, tried to be "good," with my attempt being overlaid on top of a much deeper conviction that I was "bad." I had to ally myself with people who were "good" in order to overcome my deep feeling that I was bad. Since I, myself, could never be good, my only chance was to hang around with people who were good. That was the other part of the pattern: I needed to be with people whom I *considered* to be good in order (at least) to have some tentative connection to Mother's approval and the lost paradise of her womb-like love.

As a result of the insight, I was able to see that much of my life's philosophy flowed out of these early decisions. My longing to be around "good people"—people who somehow carried the possibility that I would be able to atone and that someday I, too, would be "good"—was part of this pattern. So I sought out those who could help me transform myself, because "I was bad." All of my later involvements with teachers and gurus—like Werner Erhard, Bhagwan Shree Rajneesh, Michael Barnett, and, yes, even my wife, Rhea Powers—stem from the patterns triggered by this early wound.

Of course, a wound centered on the first emotional separation from Mother serves us by setting into motion a whole string of events that eventually allows us to function in this world as individuated human beings. If the emotional separation from the mother doesn't take place, our development is thwarted. Our potential resources will never fully incarnate.

We thus must separate from Mother psychically and emotionally as well as physically if our full potential is to have the opportunity to manifest. And so the unconscious will orchestrate delivery of the wound. Sometimes the wound is dramatic. At other times, the wound itself is not so dramatic—like a mother telling her little boy not to play with his penis—but the experience for the child is severe nonetheless.

Through this event in Santa Fe in 1992, I discovered one of the major unconscious dynamics of my psyche. It explained to me my wish to be alone and my experience of myself as an alien in a world in which I didn't belong. I became conscious of my deep belief that I am bad and of my constant struggle to try to be good, which is overlaid on that belief.

The deep intimacy and trust in my marriage with Rhea allowed me finally to look at this wound and the patterns it activated. I could see how the wound had served me. For one thing, it drew me as a child to the Christian religion in an attempt to find forgiveness and redemption for my assumed "badness." And although I left the dogmas and patterns of the Christian church behind as an adolescent, I did gain a taste of the transcendental through my contact with traditional religion. That was the beginning of my attraction to the realm of the spiritual, which later brought me into my life's work. So, by trying to be "good" in response to the feeling that I had done something terrible and unforgivable, I was actually generating the energy and the drive that led me into fulfilling my destiny.

The deep, unconscious feeling that I am bad also served me when it drove me to compensate by trying to be perfect in most of the things I did. I tried to be perfect as a ballet dancer, as a massage therapist, as a meditator, and as a spiritual therapist. In these capacities, with the skills I acquired in my search for perfection, I have served many people. I gave audiences enjoyment as a dancer. I gave my clients deep relaxation and healing as a massage therapist. And as a seminar leader, I have touched thousands of people deeply. All of this was motivated by my reactions to a wound.

The conclusion I reached as a three-year-old—that I was on my own, that I was alone—made me start to look at the world around me with different eyes . . . with wounded eyes, more aware eyes. I realize now that at that moment, I actually started to see things in terms of the need for conscious survival. I knew I must have my parents in order to survive, and

I believed that I always had to adjust my behavior in order to get them to keep taking care of me.

I wanted, therefore, to understand myself and to understand how I related to others. True, this was mainly a strategy to survive and to avoid another wounding, yet it did create greater consciousness. Ultimately it led to my ability to "read" what others wanted from me. The ability to tune in to others, to see what they wanted of me, helped me develop the ability to read people's body language, facial expressions, and voice patterns, and to recognize what was happening inside them. That awareness now serves me in my work as a seminar leader.

I avoided intimate relationships for many years due to feeling that I was alone and due to having had the experience that love hurts. Thus, during the many years when others were creating families and building their lives, I roamed the world trying to unravel the secrets of my soul. This gave me a much vaster understanding of the different conditions in which people live and work, and it now serves me powerfully in my calling. None of that would have happened had I stayed in my hometown and started a family, as most of my contemporaries did. Only when I met Rhea was I ready to fully open to deep intimacy in relationship.

I see now that most of my life's philosophy, my need to be independent and strong, and my deep convictions that we are all alone and have to fight our "battles" alone had their source in these early decisions based on this "Lone Ranger" pattern.

My upset with Rhea and the consequent resolution is a perfect example of taking back one's projections. I was convinced that my ideas of life were how life really was. I see now, however, that I overlaid an attitude, namely the "Lone Ranger" pattern, onto life. Now, as this overlay dissolves, I am finding that a much different spectrum of experiences is available to me. In the face of my relationship with Rhea, the Lone Ranger has ridden off into the sunset and on the opposite horizon I sense a new day dawning.

To summarize: what started out as an upset with Rhea, an upset I first blamed totally on her, presented me with the opportunity to become aware of decisions within aspects my psyche of whose existence I was completely oblivious. Because I was finally able to move beyond the surface and look at the dynamics behind the upset—and, in the end, not give in to my reactivity—I was able to bring to consciousness various patterns that had been unconsciously determining my life in a major way.

My conclusion is that if we can accept our personal pain, particularly as it surfaces in relationship, and not succumb to our reactivity; if we can stay within the parameters of a committed relationship and bear the uncomfortable times; we can gain invaluable insights into the mystery of who and what we really are. Then we will be able to appreciate life and its gifts much more profoundly. In the end I am stunned by the overwhelming perfection of what is.

Rhea

Here is my side of the above incident:

Something was definitely up. The surface of our relationship was so easily disrupted that something had to be brewing at a deeper level. In a way it was not surprising that our own stuff was starting to surface. When we are working, particularly in the intimacy and intensity of a group situation, our own issues are usually put aside as we focus on dealing with others. We find, therefore, that we must create a time specifically for ourselves, so whatever has been reactivated for us in the seminars or in our lives can surface. This way we also give ourselves the opportunity to integrate whatever new awarenesses have come up during the seminar work. And yet, despite our knowing that our own issues will appear as soon as we slow down, when our own patterns and shadow material do start struggling to the surface of our consciousness, they are always, at least initially, unwanted guests. "Where'd you come from? This is my time off! You get out of here!"

So, there we were in Santa Fe, with the idea that we could now relax, catch up on the latest movies, be with friends, work on this book, and have some time to be alone. Usually our time off is an occasion for our personal levels to come out and play, to reconnect, to have plenty of time to make love, play tennis, take a bike ride, and just enjoy being together. This time however, instead of relaxing and having fun together, we seemed to be tiptoeing across a minefield. Every little misstep set off an explosion. What was up? I noticed that I was feeling judged and criticized by Gawain. I felt as if everything I did was wrong. I kept trying to approach him, to connect with him, and I kept doing it in a way that did not produce the result I thought I wanted. I watched myself set up circumstances in which I knew he was likely to get upset—wanting to cuddle or talk when he was in the middle of watching a football game, wanting attention when he was sitting and having a conversation with his friends; or I was sarcastic and generally unaccepting, unloving, and critical, which was (naturally!) exactly the way I thought he had been behaving recently toward me.

Generally speaking, nothing he did was enough for me, either, and I kept having negative and destructive thoughts about him and about the relationship. I noticed the energy of those thoughts as being rather manic and out-of-control, and I knew something was moving inside me. Yet I couldn't stay centered long enough to step out of the cycle. I felt myself wanting something from Gawain, trying to get it, and not being satisfied with the result. Next I would begin to criticize him, withdraw, and feel lonely in my self-imposed isolation, then approach him again so he would make me feel better. I knew I was going through that cycle over and over, and I couldn't disconnect from it.

This had been happening for a couple of days when the incident Gawain describes above occurred—when I came home and he said he'd masturbated with a sex video and I got angry.

This issue of his enjoying sex magazines and sex videos had been with us for years and I was happy we were at a point where it was out in the open. Even though I didn't particularly like the fact that he watched sex videos, I felt I had accepted it long ago. Also, after seven years of living in Europe, I found that the European attitude toward nudism and sex had shifted my own approach to these subjects, so what once might have aroused my righteous indignation is now well within my perception of ordinary behavior.

In the past, if Gawain hid his use of a sex video or a sex magazine or, worse, if he lied about it, the perpetration/withhold mechanism came into play and he would set me up to do something he could get upset about, which then justified his lying or withholding. That established a cycle I found much more difficult to deal with than the truth.

I knew it was not just his having watched the video that triggered my emotion. So, given that this was old territory—we had the videos in the house and I knew he occasionally watched them when I went out—why was I so upset? I lay down, closed my eyes, started relaxing with my breath, and asked myself that question. Within seconds I was crying. How could "I" have a husband who did that? What about the ideal marriage I dreamed of as a young girl? Here we were, writing a book on relationship, and we had this kind of issue. What if someone found out? What would people think? How could he love me if he did "that"? These thoughts were connected to my upset, although I could feel that they were not the source of my emotion. Still, my pain was real and my tears continued to flow.

When Gawain came in, attempting to make contact, I was still upset and thought perhaps if I worked in the garden for a while, I could settle down and see what was causing all the emotion.

Because I wasn't available for contact, we really had a blowup. He said he was leaving—one of his patterns which is almost guaranteed to reactivate my own strongly developed abandoned child aspect. It did. There was a scene—the dialog sounding like a bad soap opera—with each of us sure we were right and that the other was the cause of the problem.

Then he left. I was devastated. When he later called from Colorado saying he was ending the relationship because he needed his freedom and then he hung up on me, I felt both helpless and hopeless. I kept asking myself, "What is this really about?" Somewhere in the middle of that sleepless night it dawned on me. "Ah-ha! Here we are working on a book about using the union with one's partner as a way to wake up to the illusions of the ego and connect with the Self, and suddenly he is talking about freedom, having his own space, needing time alone, having no agreements or restrictions, and feeling like he is in a prison. Now what part of him could be talking?"

I actually started laughing. It was so obvious that I couldn't believe I hadn't seen it sooner. His ego was threatened. After months of intimacy and harmony, we were actually putting our experience of union down in print. By writing this book we were taking a stand in describing something the ego wants to avoid—union, loss of control, and loss of its own separate identity. Of course, his ego would want to get the hell out of there. Since I was clearly a part of the upset, I knew my ego was also involved. Part of me would have loved to call off the relationship and the book and go back to the safe ground of being the victim of yet another man. I had a good story; surely my girlfriends would agree with me over lunch. I would be "right" and righteous—and alone.

All of that became so obvious to me that I was able to stay centered when Gawain returned, even though he was not as amused by my insight as

I was. The breathing session in which he allowed me to support him touched me very deeply. How similar we all are, I realized for the thousandth time. I had seen the same pain and heard the same decisions from so many individuals in so many different cultures during my sixteen years of working as a spiritual therapist. I was moved by Gawain's courage in facing his unique version of a pain that so many of us carry.

Once Gawain saw what had been going on between us underneath the surface, the tension relaxed for a few days and we decided to pack up our notes and the laptop computer we use for our writing, head for Colorado together, and work on the book there. I was aware that while he had seen his side of what happened, I still had not seen why I created the upset or why I had been so reactivated. I was tempted to think that everything was his creation and that I was just a supporting player in his drama. Unfortunately, I knew better. Something was still brewing in me, but it wasn't close enough yet to the surface to become conscious.

Sure enough, about an hour into Colorado, I started a fight. I actually watched myself say something I was sure would upset Gawain. Then I watched myself play innocent and reasonable as he got more and more agitated. Before long, we were back where we had been a few days before— the only difference being that this time we were both in Colorado and he was threatening to go back home! I recognized clearly that I had set this one up; but, again, I couldn't find a way out. We managed to put the upset aside long enough to rent a small apartment in a hotel, have dinner, and struggle through a long, silent evening.

I felt hopeless. I could not extract myself from the quagmire of emotion, reaction, defensiveness, attack, and withdrawal. I went to sleep asking for a dream that would disclose what was really happening inside me.

I woke up in the middle of the night with this phrase running through my head: "I can never be happy because I am bad." Whoa! Where did that come from? I remembered what I asked for as I went to sleep and recognized the words in my head as a gift from my unconscious. I slipped out of bed, went into the living room, found my pen and a pad of paper, and started writing. I tried to stay in a sleepy state so as not to lose touch with what was surfacing from my unconscious and get stuck in the chatter of my mind.

I wrote that phrase at the top of my pad of paper. "I can never be happy because I am bad." I relaxed, moving further into a sort of sleepy, soft focus as I looked inside, and then I let the words flow across the page in a stream-of-consciousness fashion. Here is what came out:

I'm bad. I am a bad person. I should never be happy. I should never have what I want because I am a bad person. I should never be successful. I should never be happy. I don't deserve to be happy. I don't deserve to have good things. I'll never be happy. I'll always be alone. No one will ever really love me because I'm bad.

Now, I ask you, with a record like that one unconsciously playing in my jukebox, what chance did Gawain (or anyone) have of getting through to me? How could I ever be deeply satisfied? How could any expression of love ever be enough? To get the love I wanted would be impossible! Now, please bear in mind that I consider myself a basically satisfied, happy, and successful person. Many people who know me well would agree. And yet, the "filter" I have just described was clearly a part of my (previously) unconscious patterning.

Since I have done a lot of this kind of work on myself—and with others, as well—I knew that the next step, after I let the stream of thoughts and decisions mentioned above run out of energy, was to find and look at the incident or moment when I first decided I was "bad."

I looked. I saw my parents arguing. I was standing in my crib and watching them. They were shouting at each other and my father walked out of the house. I have seen that moment before when I worked on myself. It was the last time I saw my father until after he and my mother were divorced, when I was two. Somehow, though, I didn't think that incident was what I was looking for, because I had already released a lot of emotion in connection with it. Then another picture popped into my mind:

I'm about four years old. I'm standing with my mother in the dining room by the radio. [Remember the days when a radio was as big as a four-year-old?] *She was angry, yelling at me. I heard myself say to her, "I'm going to go and live with my daddy." Then I saw her hand reach out, I felt the slap on my face, and I heard the fatal words: "Your daddy doesn't want you and I don't, either. You're a bad girl!"*

Even at this moment, as I write those words, I still feel pressure in my chest. Sitting in that Colorado hotel room in the middle of the night as I consciously remembered that incident for the first time, I started sobbing. I didn't think I was capable of feeling that much pain. I thought my chest would burst.

I forced myself to stay with it, to breathe into the emotion until it had run its course. Clearly, the four-year-old could not have handled that pain. It was too much. The little girl felt like she would be annihilated, like she would explode. Even on that day, almost a half-century later, I still felt as if I would burst into a billion atoms under the pressure of the pain.

In fact, in a way, I *was* annihilated as I experienced that pain. *That suppressed pain held a part of my identity together*, and after experiencing it and releasing it, I was no longer the person I had been. In that moment I was transformed. That is one of the ways transformation happens. All the energy that was tied up in the pain and in the mechanisms I used to avoid experiencing the pain was suddenly freed up and available for living life.

As Gawain mentioned above, children usually blame themselves for anything "bad" that happens between themselves and their parents. For the little one to make the decision (as I had) that "my daddy doesn't love me because I'm bad" is easier than simply facing the thought "my daddy doesn't love me." Not being loved is somehow easier if it happens for a reason, even if that reason involves great pain for the self. Taking it on and feeling justified by one's own failing is easier than dealing with the bare thought that one is simply not loved. For myself, I can see that I was protecting my image of my father by *justifying* why I was not loved. His not loving me *because I was bad* somehow made him right. It protected him. It made him okay and me the one at fault. That was easier to handle. Children love their parents so much and are so dependent on them for their own survival that they will do anything to make the parents right.

When I actually allowed myself to feel the pain of the bare thought "my daddy doesn't love me," it was excruciating. I cried like a four-year-old. Or rather, the four-year-old finally experienced and expressed the pain she had been holding for so long. When the sobs subsided, I went back to bed and snuggled up to Gawain. He rolled over in his sleep and held me. All of the evening's upset had disappeared.

In the morning we were totally back in harmony. We had two lovely days in the Colorado mountains before returning to Santa Fe. The relationship had transformed. Gawain was no longer making me wrong—which is to say, I no longer needed him to mirror my unconscious thought that I was bad—and I once again gratefully experienced him as my perfect mate for the game of waking up. Since then, while he occasionally watches a sex video alone, I no longer experience his behavior as a statement about my worth. Though I'm still not entirely comfortable with it, I don't have an issue with it, either.

A couple of days after we got back to Santa Fe, I gave a counseling session to a friend. Normally I no longer work privately with people, but this friend had been in a car accident, so I suggested that we get together to see if we could discover the dynamics at play under the apparent "accident." The techniques I used with her were the kind I used for years when I had a private practice. In this case, I guided her into a relaxed state of consciousness and took her into the pain in her body to see what the accident was echoing.

As soon as she was lying down and I started to tune in, I was flooded with information about her. Although I often "channel" (which, for me, simply means tuning deliberately in to transpersonal states of consciousness), the flood of information that filled my awareness was much more detailed and in-depth than I was used to. Forces surrounding the young woman personified themselves as guides and teachers. I was amazed at the depth and scope of the information that was available to me. I had also done a session with another friend two weeks earlier, so I could easily compare what was available now with what was available two weeks earlier and what was available years before that. There was a very distinct difference. I must confess that I was tempted to forget about the session and begin exploring the psychic realms that were opening to my inner experience. I had to remind myself that a person was lying in front of me waiting to continue the session.

I was dazzled by this new opening. Then I remembered that a few days before I had released so much old pain and I recognized that this inner opening was related to my finally having allowed myself to experience all of that emotion. Years before, while working with the *est* organization, I was struck by the fact that many of the people who participated in the organization's seminars, which were basically psychological in focus, later became very interested in exploring their spirituality. At the time, I had a feeling there was a relationship between clearing out emotional and psychological trauma and opening to the spiritual ranges of experience. Now I was certain that my recent experience of clearing out personal trauma created the space for greater transpersonal awareness.

Gawain

To stick with a relationship out of a deep commitment to awakening is to discover that one's partner is an unfathomable mystery. I was in bed with Rhea one morning and we were discussing the upset we described above. When Rhea dissected my behavior with amazing accuracy, I felt myself beginning to pull back. We had been lying in each other's arms before, but now I sat up and wrapped my arms around my legs. She commented on my body language, and I got agitated.

I had a familiar thought: "I always have to be a certain way for her." I got up and left the bedroom, thinking, "Whatever I do is never enough. Forget it, I am not busting my balls anymore for this relationship, when no matter what I do, it is not acknowledged and appreciated. It is hard enough as it is." That's one of the usual soap-opera monologues which runs through my head in moments of pain or crisis.

Within minutes, I recognized a familiar mechanism at work. I knew I was doing what I have seen others do. I knew I was using Rhea to avoid feeling my pain.

When we first fall in love, we think being with this particular person is the answer to our hopes and dreams. We think he or she will make us happy. We think he or she is the answer to our desire not to feel our pain. We have the feeling of being somehow rescued from life. (Much of this is not conscious, of course.) The knight, the princess, has finally arrived. Then the moment our pain begins to show up (which is inevitable), we often feel betrayed and we defend against feeling it.

That defense usually takes the form of fighting with our partner, thinking he or she is the source of our pain. We want our partner to be a certain way or not to be a certain way so our own pain isn't touched. We attempt to avoid the pain our partner's behavior triggers in us by having him or her be different. This is the source of much criticism of a partner in relationship.

Why do we want our partners to be different? Because their behavior frequently touches our pain and we want them to stop it immediately, so we do not have to feel what we are feeling. This creates an elaborate manipulative strategy that often plays out in relationships. Sometimes the manipulation of a partner's behavior is subtle. Sometimes it is more direct. In either case, the attempt to avoid the discomfort of one's own pain is triggered by the partner's "offensive" behavior. That is exactly what I was doing with Rhea.

As I saw all of this about myself, my avoidance structure collapsed and so did my irritation. I went back into the bedroom. And, of course, the pain I tried to avoid by blaming Rhea and leaving the room reappeared. I bent over to embrace her and had the most amazing realization. As I was hugging her, I could suddenly see that who I was *attempting* to hug was the good mother, the good Rhea, the part who would save me from my own deep feeling of being unworthy and "bad." Then, in a flash, my perception of Rhea changed. I suddenly had a sense of all of her known and unknown aspects, a sense of her totality.

My pain disappeared. I saw again, in a much deeper way than before, that in a relationship, I had—all of us have—the opportunity to wake up, to see without the veils of our preferences, without our strategies to avoid personal pain. We have the opportunity to recognize that the partner is a profound mystery, an astonishingly complex expression of life, who can be appreciated instead of changed or manipulated. In that moment, as I embraced Rhea, I suddenly understood wholeness as never before and I appreciated her as a wonderful human being with an incredible range of potentials for expressing the life force. I saw that only in appreciating her in this complete way could I experience who she really is and thus experience who *I* really am. Such a perspective is light years away from the tug-of-war that results from the avoidance-of-pain game.

The vibrant confrontation with oneself that is available in an intimate relationship can be an opening into an appreciation of life and of oneself that is unavailable virtually anywhere else. I am convinced that without the intensely alive experience of a relationship, these insights would have been much more difficult for me to experience. Very few other situations in life provide such an arena for awakening.

If you are committed to waking up, avoiding your major issues is much harder when you are in a relationship than when you are alone. In relationship, you are confronted with yourself over and over again. If you are willing, you can pass through this threshing floor into complete self-awareness and appreciation of the mystery of life.

Rhea

I believe this period in history, as we near the end of the millennium, is a time of clearing things out—both for humanity as a whole and for each of us as individuals. Many people find that even the smallest unresolved issues seem to be surfacing, so they can be looked at and released. Perhaps you have noticed in your own life that the rough edges appear to be getting sanded down. I certainly have in my life. Here, for example, is a previously unresolved issue that almost slipped by me. I was totally unaware that this seemingly simple circumstance was in charge of me.

Gawain had finished his part of this book. The next step was up to me. I didn't mind working on the book alone as long as he was also working—in the office, in the house, it didn't matter. As long as I was not the only one working. If he started watching television or listening to music, I got irritated. I talked to him about how distracting his "playing" was when I had to "work." I told him he would be more supportive of "our" project if he were working at my side, even if he couldn't work on the book at that moment. I was very reasonable, very logical, and I was certainly persuaded that my cause was just.

Gawain was basically understanding, but when he ran out of things to do around the house, he said I'd just have to handle working alone. I got upset. I got righteous. I played martyr. Gawain shrugged and told me it was my problem, and went for a ride on his bicycle. Now I was really pissed off.

Since I was working on the book and the material we are writing about was at the forefront of my consciousness, I stopped and asked myself the obvious: "What is this upset really about?" Woosh! Scenes from the past flooded my mind's eye. I was a young girl with lots of household chores to do. My friends, who didn't have so many chores, came and called me to come out and play. Time after time, my mother said, "You can't play until

155

your work is done." I would stand by the dining room window ironing and watch my friends playing in the street in front of our house. I never realized how much that hurt.

A deeper pain was present, however. It was associated with a pattern I carry that was already much too familiar—the "outsider" pattern. In this instance, it was symbolized by my standing at the window watching the other kids have a good time playing together outside. Many of us experience that we "don't belong," and so did I. I felt this pattern very strongly in my family. Both of my parents remarried after having been divorced when I was young. Both of them had a "second family" with their new spouses. I didn't feel I belonged in either my mother's new family or my father's new family. It was the "outsider" pattern, and it was very painful.

Even though this outsider pattern has been difficult for me to carry, I am aware that it has served me. This pattern supported me in developing self-reliance and a sense of connection to the transpersonal ranges of consciousness. I would even venture to say that the pain associated with this outsider pattern has also motivated me to create my own "family" through our seminars, and perhaps that has also served others. Even if they are painful for us, our patterns serve Life.

If, prior to the insight, someone had asked me if I carried pain because my mother didn't let me go out and play until I helped around the house, I probably would have been insulted. And yet here I was, interacting with Gawain on the basis of that suppressed pain. In his example above, Gawain noticed for himself how he had tried to get me to change my behavior so he could avoid being confronted with his own pain. I did the same thing. If he had listened to me and worked alongside me, as I so "reasonably" suggested, I would never have had to experience the discomfort I felt while working alone as he "played." The pain from the past would have remained buried in my unconscious. But clearly, this old pain wanted to surface, so my psyche set the stage for it to come into awareness.

We are all trying to wake up. We will create exactly the circumstances we need in order to become conscious of who and what we are. We are *not* victims. Over and over again, I am embarrassed to realize that every time I get upset with someone or some incident in my outer reality, it is because my own inner material is getting reactivated.

Gawain

This section has described and pointed to ways you can use your reactivity to bring your previously unconscious inner patterns—your shadow material—to consciousness. Indeed, beginning to recognize that your reactivity is an indicator of what is inside of you rather than a bona fide reaction to what is outside of you is a stretch. And yet it is such an indicator. That which "plugs you in," which "pushes your buttons," is attempting to give you the gift of self-knowledge. Your reactivity—to events, circumstances, or other people—is one of the ways you can begin to know those parts of your psyche that are hidden from your conscious awareness.

What upsets you in your partner is yours. True, it may also be your partner's, but that is not the point. If you are interested in using your relationship to wake up rather than simply unconsciously running your patterns (yet again!), you must begin to embrace your own reactivity, recognizing it as one of the greatest tools available to you for enhancing self-awareness.

In addition to the pointing finger mentioned above, dreams are another way one can begin to become conscious of one's shadow material.

We understand a dream to be a bridge between the unconscious and the conscious life of the dreamer. (We will discuss dreams from the point of view of you, the reader, as though you are working with your own dreams. Of course, the same observations apply when you are working with the dreams of someone else.) When you are able to read the symbolism in your dreams, you can get an idea of some of the deeper dynamics that are active in your psyche. Everything that shows up in your dream, whatever it may be—a house, your father, your mother, Jesus Christ, an ant, a policeman, etc.—can be seen as a representation of your inner energies. Usually you are not aware of the forces symbolized by the images in your dream, as they represent unconscious material.

The mind translates the forces active in you into images. The images that surface in a dream will be specific to you, the dreamer; they come from your "image library." What is contained in this image library is determined by the culture you grew up in—both your personal environment and life experiences and the collective content of your society. This latter consideration is very important. Earlier in this book, for example, Rhea mentioned a man from Ghana named Bodan. We worked with one of his dreams in our Relationship Training and were treated to a very different set of symbols from those that usually appear in the dreams of the Europeans we have worked with.

It is important to recognize that the images that arise in your dream emerge out of billions of possibilities. Why did you have those images and not others? That is significant and is one of the things we focus on when working with dreams. Looking at how the images in the dream relate to your patterns and personal circumstances can give you valuable insights regarding the intentions of the deeper forces that are active within you. Once these forces become conscious, you can choose to align with them—with those energies and intentions—instead of unconsciously trying to resist them.

Sometimes a dreamer receives a dream that not only has personal implications, but also speaks of the deeper forces active in the clan/group/ race or society the dreamer lives in. The American Indian shaman, Black Elk, received such a dream during the last century. His dream and the implications it carried for the future of his people are eloquently described in the book, *Black Elk Speaks*. Though every message may not always be as dramatic as the one Black Elk received, dreams can foreshadow all kinds of developments for the collective in which the dreamer lives.

The following dream of mine—which I had in the summer of 1992—is an example of one that contains personal meaning as well as collective implications. It is an essential dream for me and I feel, in some ways, that it also touches something essential for most men.

In the opening scene in the dream, I am in the living room of my apartment in an apartment house. (In the dream, this is where I live, although in reality I live in a house.) With me in the room are three lizards. Two of them are about six feet high when standing on all four legs. The third one is much smaller than the two others, about four feet high when on all-fours. In addition to the lizards, some people whom I don't know are in the room.

I notice that one of the big lizards wants to eat the smaller lizard. (Although in the dream the creatures seem civilized, I know that underneath their outer demeanor they really aren't. Their presence is menacing.)

Suddenly the lizard that has its eye on the smaller one jumps at it, opens its mouth very wide, and begins to swallow the smaller lizard. However, it can't get all of the smaller lizard into its mouth, and part of the body sticks out of the larger lizard's mouth.

I am utterly terrified and fear for my life. I run to the door. As I run, I notice that I am on an upper floor. I see the stairs leading downward and take them. The house is a very shabby place.

As I run down the stairs, a man carrying a gun runs past me up the stairs. Another man, who also has drawn a gun, is running up the stairs after the first man. I feel shocked and confused at that point in the dream. I turn around and run back up the stairs after the gunmen, afraid they might come into the apartment and kill someone.

Those are the dream images. What message does this dream contain for me and—perhaps—for a majority of men? Let's review its elements. (Please note that dreamwork is not an exact science. One approaches a dream through the intuition. Before working on a dream, Rhea and I always center and call up that part of ourselves that is connected to the intuitional ranges and can interpret dreams. Thus, as we move through my interpretation of these images, we invite you to accept whatever feels right to you.)

The dream starts with my being in an apartment with three lizards of two different sizes. The lizards make me uneasy. That I am in an apartment and not, for example, in a single-family house or a hut or a castle points to two things. (1) The apartment, in a building which contains other apartments, can be seen as a symbol of myself. It suggests a compartmentalization of my psyche, with parts that are walled off from other parts and unknown to each other. This indicates that there are arenas of Being in which I don't feel at home or of which I am not yet aware. (2) An apartment house, as a place of collective living (rather than an individual house), indicates that what is being expressed in the dream may have meaning for more than just myself. It may also have meaning for the collective I live in and am part of.

The action of the dream is happening in the living room (rather than the kitchen or bathroom), which indicates a pattern related to my social life, or the way I express myself and interact in the social arena. For example, if the events had happened in the kitchen, one might assume that whatever is being displayed has to do with the part of my psyche that is connected to nourishing or being nourished, that involves the life force and the way I connect with it.

I experience the lizards as threatening. What is being introduced at this point in the dream is another energy. Remember that the images contained in a dream represent internal forces within the psyche of the dreamer. The lizards, however, do not represent a human energy; they are reptiles, meaning they are cold-blooded. That description itself gives you an idea of what part of my psyche is being represented here. The lizards symbolize an aspect of me that is not social, that doesn't share society's values, that is cold-blooded and devouring.

The lizard is a primordial, archetypal energy that I associate with a dark aspect of the feminine. That they are lizards, a species much older than *Homo sapiens*, points to a pattern that is ancient compared to human beings. Steven Spielberg has tapped into the collective fear of the dark feminine in his movie *Jurassic Park*. Why has that movie earned more money than any film in the history of the world? Because it touched something deep in the collective psyche. We suggest that for the deep psyche, the dinosaurs in the film are indeed symbols of the dark feminine and that the movie/myth gives us the opportunity to confront our fear of and fascination with that force in a safe way.

The next scene in the dream—when one lizard starts to devour the other one—provides a vivid idea of what else is going on. The lizard, being so clearly primitive, depicts that which precedes all social structures and roles. Thus, what the lizard represents is an aspect of me, but I see it as separate from myself and I am afraid of it. This is indicated by the fact that I am watching it from outside rather than actually being the lizard in the dream. In other words I am not identified with the "lizard" aspect of my psyche. And it terrifies me. (In my outer life, this energy and power are hidden and I do not consciously claim them.)

In the dream, this primordial feminine energy is about to swallow one of its own—one that is smaller, weaker—and I am terrified by it. As I attempt to flee this devouring aspect of the feminine, two men with drawn guns are coming up the stairs. The guns, which I see as phallic symbols, here clearly illustrate the aggressive way the male attempts to deal with the threat of being overwhelmed by the devouring aspect of the feminine. Seen from a collective point of view, my reactions in the dream can be an indication of where maleness finds itself at this point in our psychological development. In the face of the awesomeness of the feminine force, which can swallow and devour, the masculine resorts to compensation. It will use brute force—pull out the guns—and present a show of strength, but it is actually compensating for feeling powerless and overwhelmed by the primordial forces of the feminine.

As is true for me, and as I have observed in many men I have worked with intimately during our seminars, men often seem to have a fear of being overwhelmed by women. The man fears being swallowed up, taken in, used, and then discarded by the feminine. This is actually something I feel most men confront throughout their lives. How do we deal with the enormous power of the feminine? This dilemma can be seen in the struggle to individuate—to cut mother's apron strings and become one's own man—or in the more abstract and usually unconscious fight of the masculine not to get lost in the expansive emptiness of the feminine.

This can be observed even at the most fundamental level of human life. Consider the sperm and the egg. A single ejaculation contains millions of sperm, all of which are racing for the woman's egg. And, except in the rare case of fraternal twins, only one of them (if that) will succeed in fertilizing the egg. If one diligent little swimming sperm does make it, the instant it penetrates the egg it is absorbed and its identity as a sperm, as the masculine, is lost. Although the egg is fertilized, the resulting embryo is initially feminine—and, in the case of a male fetus, it stays feminine until the mother's body releases a hormone which shifts its sex and makes it masculine. Maleness thus comes about due to a differentiation of the fetus from its essential femaleness.

Perhaps we all carry some residual cellular memory of that primary experience—as if men know that to fully embrace the feminine means the dissolution of their identity. We are threatened by the forces of the vast feminine. As the dream indicates, we are afraid we will be swallowed by that primordial energy. And we are right. We will, sooner or later, have to let go of our identity as separate entities and open to the formless, and through that conscious opening enter a new stage of our development, one that is not dominated by resistance to this process.

If, as a man, you have identified with your masculine aspects, you can use your partner to open the doors to your feminine forces. In this way, you can transcend your self-image and open to the fullness of your Being.

161

15

RHYTHMS AND CYCLES

L ife is cyclical. Life undulates and flows through time, weaving us into
its patterns as it will. The twists and turns of life often bring us back to
familiar scenes we thought were long behind us. Most of us, however, tend
unconsciously to think of life as something that moves straight ahead, that
proceeds inexorably toward a certain future destination. The mind perceives
life as if it were a road leading toward something. Clearly, there are people
who have no sense of destination and act as though life is what happens to
them while they are waiting to die. But most of us seem to perceive life as
moving toward social acceptance, material wealth, a fulfilling relationship,
a satisfying profession, political power, spiritual enlightenment, wisdom, or
any other goal that is a symbol of what we think life is about. We do certain
things in a sequential order, hoping to achieve the goal we have set for
ourselves. While attempting to reach our goal, we are beset by worries, by
our hopes and fears about achieving the goal. As if that isn't stressful
enough, once we do feel we have achieved our goal, then we may start
worrying about losing what we have gained.

We also tend to see illness, divorce, financial difficulties, and other of
life's "problems" as interruptions in our journey toward what we perceive
life to be about. Rarely do we perceive these "disruptive" events as integral
to the flow of life. Rarely are we awake enough to recognize these events as
part of the fulfillment of our destiny rather than as hindrances to that
fulfillment.

We seldom stop to realize that life is not a process which begins with
our birth and ends with our death. Life was here before we were born and
will continue after we die. Nor is it a completed process—it is continually
changing and evolving. Life is inherently incomplete and in process. Life

163

was in process when we were born and will continue its own process after we are gone. Life moves in rhythms and cycles. It is forever becoming, existing, and dissolving. Life can't be put in a box.

That is difficult for those of us who like to have a tidy, final answer to whatever we are grappling with. Life will always be imperfect, because it is always unfinished. It will always elude the perfectionist's claim to have it all figured out. The wish for perfectionism is just another expression of and attempt to control. Since we are parts of life, expressions of the life force, we are also bound to the cyclical, undulating nature of life. When we perceive life as an undulation rather than as a line that goes from one place to another, we notice that things have a way of appearing, existing, disappearing, and returning. Love has a way of appearing, disappearing, and returning. In relationship, it is important to remember that our experience of the energy we call love, the experience of connectedness, waxes and wanes as does everything else.

Life has a flow to it. As we find the courage to relax and release ourselves into that flow rather than attempting to structure and control everything, we relax into ourselves and into our essential relatedness with life. This experience of our relatedness to the natural forces, to the flow of life, is often lost when we have a goal-oriented perception of life. In fact, our relatedness to the rhythms of life is a part of us we have sacrificed as we have become civilized. Various native cultures around the globe have managed to maintain their experience of relatedness with life, and they have much to offer us in this regard. There is something to the fact that Australian Aboriginals call themselves "Real People" and refer to civilized whites as Mutants; and that the Indians of the Colombian Andes refer to the white race as Little Brothers, while seeing themselves as the race of the Elder Brothers. The growing contemporary interest in shamanism reflects our desire to reconnect with the natural forces. It represents a step away from the goal-oriented perception of life and an opening to the mystery of the interrelatedness of all life, an interrelatedness that transcends both time and space. The worldwide ecological movement is also, of course, a response to our alienation from the very nature that sustains our life.

Within the cyclical, undulating nature of life, the experience of love comes and goes. Although we know (at least intellectually) that ultimately everything is a vibration called unconditional love, the way this energy is

164

actually expressed and experienced does not necessarily always fit the image of what Western society calls love. At times, partners may feel withdrawn or angry, or their focus may be centered on some unidentified inner process instead of being directed lovingly toward their mate. If you have a linear perception of reality, you may feel distraught when the nature of your partner's interaction with you shifts. You may think that things were good and now they have turned bad. You may think all is lost, that the love is gone, that your relationship is over.

If, on the other hand, you are in touch with the cyclical nature of reality, you can relax. You get close, then you move apart as other aspects of your psyche claim your attention, and then you get close again. You and your partner are connected through the rhythms and cycles of life. When you experience this fact, you will be able to give your partner space for his or her process. Something in you will know and trust the cyclic, always-returning nature of the experience we call love.

Truly opening to the flow of life brings you to surrender. As you recognize that life is moving through you with its rhythms and cycles, just as the seasons move through nature, you begin to relax. You begin to trust. You start to experience your partner as an ever-flowing expression of the life force, just as you are. Out of this experience, space will be created within you—space to let your partner be the way he or she is expressing right now, and also space for you to move through the rhythms and cycles of your own nature.

We can all identify with Charles Schultz' "Peanuts" cartoon some years ago which showed Lucy musing, "Why do there have to be ups and downs? Why can't there just be ups and ups?" Ups and downs are part of life. However when we relax into life's own rhythm, we feel a renewed sense of the sacredness life and the blessing of love in all of its guises.

Through trust and surrender we gain access to our essential Self. That Self is the life force incarnate. Through this deep and intimate connection to Self, we begin to see ourselves not as singular, struggling individuals, but as organisms that are connected to an even bigger organism, parts within a larger whole. When we fully experience this, surrender happens naturally. We give in and let go. We become one with the flow of life. And our partner can be the catalyst which leads us to this realization.

The way our relationship manifests on the outer levels at any given moment doesn't affect this deeper truth. Our partner is an expression of the life force incarnate, just as we are. By embracing our partner as he or she is, we embrace life as it is.

Most of us are still very young in our understanding of life. Like children, our focus, collectively and individually, remains fixed on ourselves. We still tend to define what is good and what is bad by our personal preferences and by our personal comfort levels. We still see the universe through the filter of our own needs and desires. We have not yet matured in our understanding and recognized the fact that life doesn't care what we want. That is to say, life does not exist to serve us—we exist to serve life. We are so busy trying to understand (read: control) life, to use life to our own ends, that we ignore the obvious evidence that such is not possible. Life uses us.

Most "New Age" spirituality is still based on the principles of the male mind. It is a form of magic. Affirmations and visualizations are an attempt to manipulate life. While it may be useful for our own clarity to state our preferences to the universe, we must remember that our preferences come from our minds. And our minds are not the highest authority in the universe. For us—Rhea and Gawain—the truest prayer is, "Not my will, but Thine be done." Techniques that attempt to control life, to make it more comfortable and manageable for us, appeal to our inner children. Often the children within us seek to control life so they are not so overwhelmed by the forces working through and around us. Life, however, cannot be controlled.

The mature parts of our psyche can attempt to discover and then align themselves with the intentions of deeper forces of the unconscious that are actually directing our life. Through an awareness of our multiplicity, through an awareness of the process of projection, by attempting to uncover our shadow, and by working with our dreams, we can get glimpses of the direction our deeper Self is headed. Then, with trust, we can surrender to the wisdom of our totality and let life live us.

16

LAST WORDS

The minute I heard my first love story
I started looking for you, not knowing
how blind I was.
Lovers don't finally meet somewhere
They're in each other all along.

–Rumi

We have discussed many ways in which consciously living in an intimate relationship can be a path of awakening. Your partner can support you as you take back your projections—if you begin to recognize that whatever you are resisting in your partner is something you are resisting in yourself. Your partner can support you in recognizing your unconscious, or shadow, material by reflecting it for you. Then, as you take back your projections and own your disowned shadow material, your experience of your totality increases and you move toward wholeness.

Many people unconsciously dramatize their pain in their relationships rather than using the Other as an opportunity to wake up. They unconsciously and mechanically re-run their patterns without ever recognizing that alternative options exist. These people attempt to use their relationship to defend against their own long-buried pain. Ultimately that defense is impossible, as the act of opening to feel one's love for another also entails opening to one's pain. You cannot open only to love. If you open to one emotion, you open to all emotions. This is why so many people choose not to open to love at any depth. Instead, they accumulate colorful, often entertaining stories about how they have been wronged by their man or how their woman done them in . . . once again. The role of the victim is so popular because it is so easy. On the other hand, there is no real satisfaction in it.

It is true that your wounds will be touched through the intimacy of a committed relationship. As long as your commitment to the relationship supports you in staying to examine your wounds rather than fleeing in an attempt to escape your pain, you can redeem your wounds by recognizing how they have served you. You can recognize how past wounds have contributed to developing your current resources. In that way, you can more consciously claim the resources and gifts you have developed. You can also begin to appreciate not only the perfection of your life, but the perfection of all expressions of the life force, as well. You can consciously shift from being a victim of life to being an ally of life. You can, with awareness, align yourself with the flow of life instead of attempting to direct or control life with the limited power of your outer mind.

Any gain in consciousness has a cost. Confronting your own long-buried wounds may be difficult, even painful. Through the process of opening yourself to love, you will also open yourself to long-buried pain. You will be confronted with aspects of your totality that are not ego-enhancing, parts of yourself that other parts of you do not like or approve of. This is the price you must pay if you are truly to know yourself. But by confronting your unclaimed pain and experiencing it, you give yourself the opportunity to release the energy of the suppressed pain that has blocked your experience of spontaneity and joy. You free yourself to live fully in the moment, because there is finally nothing from the past against which you must defend.

Not wanting to confront that pain is natural. It is possible that the resistance to confronting your pain is based on a deeper knowledge that you do not yet have the resources to deal with the pain. If that has kept you from moving deeper into relationship, the insights and techniques in this book, particularly the heart centering technique, may support you in finding within yourself the resources to confront whatever is in the way of your having the relationship you want.

As Rumi wrote, your partner is within you because your partner is a part of you. He or she represents a part of your totality. This is the gift of relationship. Through your partner, you can come to know aspects of yourself that would otherwise remain hidden from your experience of who you are. Living consciously in an intimate relationship can support you in awakening to the essence of your Being. Your partner can be the mirror in which you finally recognize your Self.

RIDING LESSONS

Exercises for Riding the Dragon

Riding Lessons

In the following section are several exercises designed to allow you and your partner to explore many different arenas of your life as individuals and as a couple. The exercises cover the spectrum of human experience from the mundane to the transcendent. There are exercises to support you in recognizing the patterns you bring to your relationships. Other exercises allow you to discover many of the different aspects that live within your inner community. Communication processes and meditation techniques are included as well.

All of the exercises are intended to give you an experience of concepts we have been discussing in this book. Enjoy!

To us, relationship in its deepest essence is an unfathomable mystery to be experienced and appreciated rather than something to conceptualize and squeeze into a prescribed set of behaviors. It is a state of being—not a series of actions to take or things to "do." And yet within the mystery, there are things you may do that, potentially, can open you more deeply to the unfolding gift of relationship. While one bows to the mystery, one can also honor those parts in oneself that seek to understand and to find some mastery in life. In that spirit, we offer you this "how-to" section. It is meant as a roadmap of routes you might like to explore as you seek to discover the deeper aspects within your relationship and within yourself.

The exercises that follow are intended to support your experience of relationship as a spiritual path. We have used them many times in our seminars and trainings, with literally thousands of people on four continents, and we know they work.

At this point, we'd like to give you a hint with regard to this work. In our seminars, we have noticed that there are two ways to approach exercises like those that follow. One way is to think about them. The other way is to do them. The difference is the same as the difference between eating the menu or eating the meal. The satisfaction is in doing the work. You can think about it later.

Sometimes thinking about something feels safer than actually immersing oneself in the experience. For the following exercises, our suggestion is— just do them! After you have had the experience then you can think about everything. Remember that whatever surfaces for you in response to the exercises is yours. The exercises are designed to prompt your unconscious to offer up its gifts to you so you can experience more of who you are.

While we appreciate that the exercises can, at times, be confronting, they are also intended to be fun and to deepen the intimacy you share with your partner. If you are not in a committed partnership or if your partner for some reason is not available to do the exercises with you, you can do them with a friend, or alone. If you are doing them alone, we suggest, for those exercises that contain a dialogue, that you use a tape recorder—first reading the relaxation process and the questions onto a tape, then playing it back and answering the questions as if someone were asking them of you. Remember to leave a pause between questions for your answers.

If you are in a relationship and are doing these processes with a partner, approaching them in the spirit of mutual discovery and adventure is useful. Yes, you do need courage to confront the uncomfortable (and perhaps unconscious) areas of your life and your relationship. But opening to each other in deeper and more intimate ways can also be a lot of fun—which is what you will experience should you venture into the processes and meditations on the following pages.

You may find the intensity generated by these processes and exercises too difficult to deal with at the present time. In that case, consider working with them when you feel more centered or in a more secure place, whether within yourself or in your relationship. Or, if you and your partner are in a crisis or a circumstance where you have difficulty remaining in your mature aspects when you interact with each other, you may find it helpful to have a third person present to facilitate the communication between you—to "keep it clean."

In any case, when you choose to enter into this work with your totality and to give it your honest intention and focus, it can be tremendously enriching—for you as an individual and for your relationship.

The Heart

Centering in the heart[*] is a central theme in our work, so we will open this section with an introduction to the heart meditation. You may wish to read through this entire section initially, then come back and read the steps one by one, as you move through the meditation.

First, find a space where you can be comfortable and uninterrupted for about twenty minutes. Begin the heart meditation by sitting in a comfortable position on the floor or in a chair, with your back as straight as possible without discomfort or tension. Take a couple of deep breaths to quiet yourself. Rest your hands gently on your knees. As you sit there, become aware of your hands. Bring the focus of your attention to your hands, energizing them with your awareness. Then, begin preparing yourself to experience the mystery of touch.

As Brugh Joy points out, and as our experience confirms, *who* is touching the body makes no difference to the deep psyche. The quality of the touch is what's important. So, prepare yourself to touch your Heart Center with the same energy and awareness with which you would compassionately comfort a young child, an elderly person, someone you love deeply, or someone in distress. The deep psyche is not concerned with personality, ideas, or concepts. The deep psyche only knows it has been touched, and it recognizes the quality of the touch. Being aware of this, you can facilitate healing for yourself by opening to the mysteries of your own inner healing aspects and moving beyond the idea that healing energy must come from outside.

Next, gently bring your hands to the heart chakra, with awareness. (This energy center is in the middle of your chest, above your solar plexus and about two-thirds of the way down the breastbone from the throat.) Place one hand over the other, so the thumbs meet. As you feel your hands touch your body, have the feeling that someone else is touching you through your hands. Perhaps it is even someone you don't know very well. Perhaps it is someone with great healing abilities.

---

[*] Based on a meditation developed by W. Brugh Joy, M.D.

Open to the flow of energy from your hands, experiencing them as if they were great balls of light and energy. Have the feeling that energy from your hands is penetrating the cells and tissues of your body. Open to it. Open to the feeling that waves of well-being are flowing through all parts of your body.

Then begin opening to the four main attributes of the Heart Center. First, open to Compassion.

Compassion. The ability to be with another in such a way that the other's experience becomes your own, while you still maintain your own sense of self. Take a breath. Feel yourself opening not only to personal compassion but also to collective compassion. Feel Compassion. Have the sensation that you are being held in Compassion. Open to the energy behind the word, the force in the universe that lies behind the concept. Compassion.

After you have felt into the experience called Compassion, begin to open to the second attribute of the Heart Center: *Innate Harmony*, your natural ability to center. This is your ability to locate your sense of self as a stillpoint of consciousness, regardless of what may be happening around or within you. It is your ability to find the calm in the midst of the storm, peace in the center of chaos.

Next, open to the third attribute of the Heart Center: *The Healing Presence*. Open to that force in the universe which can heal, harmonize, heighten, and attune all levels of your own Beingness. Open also to your own ability to transmit or channel this healing force to yourself, to others, and to this planet. Feel that energy filling you and feel that it is available to you and to others through you.

And last, open to *Unconditional Love*: love that does not have to be deserved or earned. Love that is beyond personal preference or personal judgment. Love that simply is. Experience it as an infinite flow of energy outflowing from your heart.

Then just sit quietly for a while longer, appreciating and repeating the four attributes of the heart, almost as if they were mantras. ("Mantra" is a Sanskrit term for sounds that, if repeated many times, can induce meditative, altered states of consciousness.) Compassion, Innate Harmony, the Healing Presence, Unconditional Love. In the beginning, the words may not have much impact on you. But as you practice this meditation, many things may happen. Your experience of the speed of your bodily functions may change.

176

You may have the feeling that things slow down—that time stops. You may have a variety of images, associations, and insights, from the mundane to the sublime. As you open to the Heart Center you may discover depths of your Being that you were never in touch with before.

Associating the attributes of the Heart Center with an image or experience in your outer life that, for you, symbolizes the characteristics associated with the Heart Center can be very useful. Perhaps you know inspirational people—either living or dead, celebrated and famous . . . or not—who represent the quality these attributes carry for you. Then when you shift into focusing on the Heart Center and you recall an image of that person or those persons, the forces they embody will come forward in your experience. Or, perhaps the association that evokes the attributes of the Heart Center for you is a scene from nature, a work of art, a piece of music, or a line of poetry or prose. Later, just recalling the images, or the scene, or the piece of music will evoke in you the experience of the forces associated with the Heart Center. This will make it easier and easier for you to experience these forces in your daily life.

The heart meditation is a very useful spiritual practice. In this transition time in the evolution of humanity, there is and will continue to be a growing amount of chaos, both in the inner and outer worlds. The development of a home base (portable!) and the ability to center will be increasingly useful as we face the coming chaos. Instead of reacting automatically to the vicissitudes of life, our having the ability to center gives us a chance to choose *which* aspect of our multiplicity will respond to a given circumstance. It gives us a chance to move consciously into our adult aspects instead of once again sacrificing the moment to the children.

Centering in the heart also helps to integrate and harmonize the lower three chakras (our involvement with physical and emotional survival on planet Earth) with the upper three chakras (which connect us to the spiritual dimensions of the human experience, the subtle awareness that we are more than a body and a mind bent on surviving in this physical form). This supports a balance between the part of us that is involved in the individual human experience and the part that is open to collective or transpersonal dimensions. The Heart Center is truly the meeting place of heaven and Earth.

Two of Hearts

Here is another heart exercise. We suggest that you read through the instructions a couple of times before beginning. Then you should be able to do the exercise without needing to refer to these pages. If you prefer, you can read the instructions onto a tape, then play it to guide you through the exercise. Playing soft, meditative music in the background throughout the exercise may help you shift your awareness from the outer levels to the inner levels.

Sit opposite your partner, so your knees are almost, but not quite, touching. Have your eyes closed, using the breath to consciously relax your body. Relax your shoulders and your jaw. Have your hands relaxed, resting on your knees, with palms facing upward. As you sit there, become aware of your body. Notice your body sensations and have the experience of breathing into how they feel at this moment. As you become aware of your body sensations, have the feeling that you open to your skeletal structure—to all of the bones in your body.

Next, open to all the muscles, ligaments, and tendons that are around your skeletal structure. Feel that. Then open to your inner organs and all of your tissues and cells. Then open to the largest of your organs, the skin that surrounds your body. Feel that—breathing gently to open to your experience.

Begin to center in the heart, opening to whatever images symbolize your experience of the mystery of the Heart Center. Then open to the basic attributes of the Heart Center—Compassion, Innate Harmony, the Healing Presence, and Unconditional Love. As you experience yourself opening to these attributes, gently lift your hands so they connect physically with your Heart Center. Allow your touch to augment and strengthen your connection with this center. Have the feeling that you consciously inhale and exhale through this center.

Then begin to open your eyes in a relaxed gaze. Just allow them to open on their own rather than opening them deliberately. By allowing them to open rather than making them open, you cause your eyes to strengthen your experience of this relaxed space instead of removing you from it.

As your eyes open, allow them to take in whatever they happen to have opened onto. Then gently shift them and gaze at your partner's Heart Center. After a minute or so, start to relax your eyes even more. Still looking at your partner's Heart Center, allow your focus to widen so, after a while, you begin to see not only the center of your partner's chest, but also his or her whole body, the surrounding area, and—when your eyes are very relaxed—parts of yourself. The center of this relaxed gaze remains the Heart Center of your partner, but your eyes are open and relaxed, so you have the experience of seeing everything and nothing in particular at the same time.

Until now your hands had been resting on your knees, palms facing upward. Now lift them a little bit, up into the air (about ten inches), so you have the experience that they are floating in front of you. The most important part of this exercise is to continue to allow your relaxed gaze to rest on your partner's Heart Center. After you have opened your hands to this new position, take a few moments to become aware of the energy around them. Perhaps you will feel they are surrounded by an electrical field; you may feel they have become very large or that they feel like big cotton balls. Just notice how it is for you.

If you feel as if nothing is happening in your hands, feel into this apparent nothing, since it also will have a certain feeling. On the experiential levels, "nothing" doesn't really exist, since even the feeling of "nothing" is a sensation one can experience. Usually the "nothing" that people report feeling is actually the result of an unfulfilled expectation. That is to say, they think they should feel something other than what they are feeling. The key to this is to sense more accurately into what *is* happening. In any case, notice what is happening in your hands. Have the experience that your hands are being supported or carried by some force. Feel them becoming very light, while still allowing your relaxed gaze to rest on your partner's Heart Center.

Then, as you remain in tune with your partner and in the same rhythm as your partner, you both lift your hands as if in slow motion until each of you is gently touching your own Heart Center. Rest your hands there for a while and then, again at the same time as your partner, allow your hands to separate and move slowly toward your knees, palms facing up. Finish the movement by having your hands gently float in front of you. Maintaining the same rhythm as your partner is a way to tune in to each other at a level beyond words. It allows you to find a synchronicity between you that transcends the outer levels of the mind. Then you operate in harmony with each other from that space.

Do this movement with your hands four more times, so you have done it a total of five times. During these movements it is important that your hands not touch your partner's hands and that your eyes remain relaxed and centered on your partner's Heart Center.

At the end of the fifth movement, bring your hands out from your Heart Center once more. Then let your hands touch your partner's hands and close your eyes. Now allow your hands to guide you. There are no further instructions for what to do with your hands. Feel into what is happening and open to whatever else spontaneously wants to happen. In this way, instead of the outer mind determining what happens, another inner, guiding principle is allowed to take over.

This exercise is a wonderful way to share the Heart Center with another human being—especially a loved one. It has the capacity to open communication beyond the mundane levels of daily life, which, though important, are far from the whole picture in the mystery of your being Spirit manifested in form. This exercise can give your relationship a nourishing vacation from the outer levels by dropping you into a deep, clear pool of Being.

How Do You Say "I Love You"?

This is a simple, fun, yet illuminating four-part exercise on nonverbal communication in a relationship. Each person writes four lists on four different pieces of paper, taking about ten minutes to complete each list. This is done separately, without discussion.

1.   First, list the things you do to demonstrate your love for your partner.

2.   Then list the things your partner does that you experience as expressions of his or her love for you.

3.   Next, list the things you do (or don't do!) to express your annoyance or lack of the experience of love for your partner.

4.   Finally, list the things your partner does (or doesn't do) that you experience as expressions of his or her annoyance or lack of the experience of love for you.

Compare your lists.

This simple exercise can show you what messages your partner is actually receiving from your actions—and vice versa. You may both be surprised to learn that the messages you think you are sending are not the ones being received.

The Secret Process
(Discovering Deeper Intimacy)

If you are keeping secrets from your partner, from others, or even from yourself, you are tying up tremendous amounts of energy that are then not available for your relationship. If you are hiding anything, you cannot afford to be spontaneous, and the possibility for real intimacy in your relationship is severely curtailed. Furthermore, by hiding things, you give them unnecessary importance. You become attached to what you are hiding and identify with it, as if it says something about who you really are. This tends to fix your sense of self and makes opening to the flow of your multiplicity and magnificence much more difficult. The following exercise will give you the opportunity to let go of what you are holding onto unnecessarily.

Before beginning this potentially reactivating process, be sure you and your partner are both willing to see it through to completion. You need not only to complete it for yourself, but also to give your partner time to complete it.

We suggest that you make an agreement with one another before you begin that you will not use the information you share in the process against each other. Agreeing not to use the information against each other in the middle of an upset is particularly important. (Although we admit that possibility will be very tempting at one time or another.)

You will find value in giving yourself time after you have done the process in *both* directions just to talk about how it was for each of you to hear what was revealed—what was hard to hear, where you wanted to laugh, what thoughts or experiences you've had that were similar to what was shared, what you already knew that the other partner thought was a secret. Those kinds of things.

In the days following the process, other reactions and thoughts may surface and you would be wise to set aside some time to share those as well, making sure you do so on an occasion when you can trust yourself to stay centered and both of you are willing to listen to each other. This process brings up a lot of vulnerability, and you really need to be willing to treat your partner—who is another soul floundering around in the mystery of being human, just as you are—with love and respect, if you are to take the process on at all.

We suggest that you not read through the process itself before doing it with your partner. However, if you do read it, know that the responses which come from inside when you are actually doing the exercise may be different from the ones which come to mind when you are merely reading it. Be willing for that to happen.

Make sure you have at least two hours for this process and that even if it takes longer, you are both committed to completing it—in both directions. Do whatever needs to be done to insure that you will not be interrupted by other people or by the telephone. Decide which partner will answer the questions first and which partner will read the questions first.

When a question is asked, the responding partner reports the first thing that comes to mind. That is important. No editing should occur. Since the purpose is to let go of any secrets or withheld information you may have kept from your partner, your deliberating and deciding what to say and what not to say would be counterproductive. Once you reach question #7 and it has been answered, the partner reading the question repeats it by asking, "What else . . . ?" until no further answers are forthcoming. In other words, you clear out everything in response to that and to each of the subsequent questions in the process.

The partner reading the questions and receiving the answers needs just to hear the answers. You must be careful not to respond with anything that could be interpreted as a judgment. Raising your eyebrows in shock, gasping, or saying something like "You did! How could you?" is not helpful. The idea is to offer a neutral space in which the secrets can be released, to give your partner the experience of being heard. The person sharing already has enough judgments of his or her own about the material, or what's being shared wouldn't be secret in the first place!

A simple nod of the head or a neutral response like "Okay" or "Fine" is useful to let the partner who is answering the questions know you have heard the response. And the listening partner *really does need to hear the answer*—needs to be present and to stay centered. Most likely, some of the responses will be reactivating to the one receiving the information. So, as the listener, you need to remain centered in an aspect of yourself that holds the context of the exercise, which is: to create space in your relationship for intimacy and spontaneity. The exercise is intended to empower your relationship, and even though receiving some of the information may be difficult, the listener must resist the temptation to switch into his or her own rejected child or judgmental parent aspect. Stay centered. Breathe!

Sit opposite your partner, holding hands, and make eye contact for a few minutes. Both of you should take a few deep breaths to let your mind go blank so you can "tune in" to each other. Then, let go of each other's hands and the partner who is presenting the process begins reading the questions. After you have read each question, once again make eye contact with your partner (and continue making eye contact as each response is presented).

Here is the process:

1.   Recall the happiest time in your childhood.

2.   Recall another happy time in your childhood.

3.   Recall an event in your childhood that you are proud of and that you have never been acknowledged for.

4.   Recall something you did as a child that nobody ever found out about.

5.   Recall the time you were most embarrassed as a child.

6.   Recall something else from your childhood that was embarrassing to you and that nobody ever found out about.

7.   What are you most afraid will happen if you reveal your secrets? (Repeat: "What else are you afraid will happen if you . . . ?" as per the instructions above.)

8.   Given your life right now, what are you hiding that you are willing to reveal? (Repeat: "What else are you . . . ?")

9.   Given your life right now, what are you hiding that you are not willing to reveal? (Repeat)

10. With regard to your professional life, what are you hiding? (Repeat)

11. With regard to your professional life, what are you hiding that you are not willing to reveal? (Repeat)

12. With regard to your professional life, what are you most afraid someone will find out? (Repeat)

13. With regard to your body, what are you hiding that you are willing to reveal? (Repeat)

14. With regard to your body, what are you hiding that you are not willing to reveal? (Repeat)

15. With regard to food, drugs, and alcohol, what are you hiding that you are willing to reveal? (Repeat)

16. With regard to food, drugs, and alcohol, what are you hiding that you are not willing to reveal? (Repeat)

17. With regard to money, what are you hiding that you are willing to reveal? (Repeat)

18. With regard to money, what are you hiding that you are not willing to reveal? (Repeat)

19. With regard to sexuality, what are you hiding that you are willing to reveal? (Repeat)

20. With regard to sexuality, what are you hiding that you are not willing to reveal? (Repeat)

21. With regard to sexuality, what is your biggest secret?

22. With regard to sexuality, what other secrets do you have? (Repeat)

23. With regard to relationship, what are you hiding? (Repeat)

24. With regard to relationship, what are you hiding that you are not willing to reveal? (Repeat)

25. What have you never told anyone? (Repeat)

26. What else would you like to take this opportunity to let go of? (Repeat)

This is the end of the process. Take a breath and relax. When you are ready, reverse roles. When you have both answered all of the questions, take time to share with each other as suggested above. The sharing is also a part of the process, so remember to stay centered and don't turn the microphone over to your inner children.

The Aspect Processes
(or: Is Anyone Else in There?)

Becoming aware of the multiplicity of your psyche is a big advantage in dealing with the mystery of being human. The following three processes are designed to reveal to you the child, adolescent, and young adult aspects that most dominate your experience and expression of life. Once you are aware of these younger aspects of your psyche and are able to recognize the strategies they employ to get along in life, you will more easily be able to open consciously to the mature aspects of your inner community and to have access to the wisdom, resources, and gifts they carry.

The Set-up

The process is done with a partner. One of you reads the exercise and the other does the exercise. We suggest that you stick to the words given here, though you may be tempted to throw in some questions of your own once you get an idea of where it's going. The exercise begins with a fairly standard relaxation process, then moves on to direct questions. When there is no direct question, no response is needed, although the partner doing the exercise may want to nod or to lift a finger during the relaxation portion to indicate readiness to move to the next stage. This feedback can help the reader not to go too fast. Because the person doing the exercise is essentially outside of time, gauging how fast to present the relaxation process may be difficult for the reader. What seems slow to the reader may be very fast for the person doing the work.

After the first two questions, the reader should repeat the questions, as indicated, until no more responses are forthcoming. For example, after hearing the response to, "How do you experience your life?" the reader will ask, "Fine, and how else do you experience your life?"—continuing until the other person has no more answers to offer.

Emotions and feelings may surface during the process. If they do, that is fine. Allow them to surface, and stay with the process. The partner reading the questions should remain neutral and continue as conditions permit. That is, the reader may need to pause, waiting until the emotion subsides before going on with the questions. But do continue. Do not get side-tracked into comforting your partner or stopping the process. Actually, the surfacing of emotions is useful. It means energy which has been held in that aspect is being released. (You may also need to consciously center, so your resistance to your own emotional material does not get in the way.)

As in any process of this type, the one who is doing the process needs to respond to a direct question by saying the first thing that comes to mind. Do not edit your response or try to get it to match any preconceived ideas. Just let it flow. Let the aspect that is speaking present itself as fully as possible. If a change occurs in voice vibration (you may suddenly find yourself speaking with the voice of a four-year-old, for example) or body language presents itself which is naturally associated with the aspect that is answering the question, so much the better. At the same time, what's there should not be exaggerated by the person doing the exercise. Just allow each aspect to present itself as authentically as possible. Note that the Child Aspect Process we suggest includes not just the child, but also the earlier stages: conception, embryonic and fetal periods, then birth, infancy, and finally childhood. If one or more of those very young aspects should appear, accept it and go through with the process. Just trust what comes up for you.

As was true with the Secret Process, it is helpful if the person reading the questions makes some neutral response when the question is answered, so the person in the process knows he or she has been heard. Something simple like, "Okay," "Uh-huh," or "Fine" is satisfactory.

You will need to allow about an hour for each person, so if you are both going to do the process, make sure you have two hours without interruption from outside sources. The person doing the process should be lying down in a comfortable position. In an exercise such as this one, in which a person enters an altered state of consciousness as a result of deep relaxation, the body's temperature will often naturally lower, so it is best to cover the person with a sheet or light blanket before beginning, to avoid distraction later on.

This process also provides practice in centering in the heart, so doing that is a good way to begin. Once you are both settled, take a few moments to center. Each of you can just close your eyes, take a few deep breaths, let go of any distracting thoughts, and center in your heart. The partner who is presenting the exercise waits for a verbal ready-sign from the person doing the process, then opens his or her eyes and begins reading the following.

The Child

With your eyes closed, imagine yourself in a room where you can feel very comfortable, very secure, and very relaxed. Take a look around the room and make sure everything is exactly the way you would like it to be. Have a place in the room to lie down. And then feel yourself lying down there and relaxing, becoming more and more comfortable.

Use your breath to allow your body to become more and more comfortable. Let go of any tension or tightness as you inhale, and release it as you exhale.

Visualize your feet, and visualize a golden liquid flowing into them through your toes. Know that everywhere this golden liquid passes, it is going to leave behind it soothing comfort, healing energy, and waves of relaxation.

Visualize the golden liquid flowing through your toes. Feel it moving soothingly and relaxingly through the muscles of your feet, up through your ankles and into your calves. Feel the golden liquid moving gently and relaxingly up through your knees and into your thighs. Consciously relax the long muscles of your thighs as the golden liquid fills your legs completely with waves of comfort and relaxation.

Then allow the golden liquid to move gently through your hips and pelvic area into your lower abdomen. Feel the golden liquid moving soothingly and relaxingly around and through the muscles and organs as it flows gently up your torso.

Allow the golden liquid to move through your solar plexus into your chest. Take a deep breath and, as you exhale, relax the muscles that surround your chest. Visualize the golden liquid flowing gently through the heart muscle, soothing and steadying your heartbeat.

Then allow the golden liquid to move up to your shoulders and begin flowing gently down into your upper arms. Allow the golden liquid to move gently down your arms, through your elbows, and down into your forearms.

Take a breath and relax. Feel the waves of comfort and relaxation moving soothingly down through your wrists, into your hands, and into your fingers. Then see the golden liquid moving gently up your neck and into your head, filling your head with waves of comfort and relaxation.

Now your body is completely filled with the soothing, relaxing, golden liquid.

Then mentally check out your body and notice if you feel any pockets of tension or tightness remaining anywhere. If you do, use your breath and visualize those tensions being dissolved into the golden liquid.

Know that this golden liquid will keep your body safe and protected, so you and you only can return to your body any time you choose. Then silently ask your own expanded consciousness to join in this process, requesting that it reveal to you the child aspect of your totality who most dominates your experience of life.

[Pause. Then continue reading:]

Take a breath and center in your heart.

Call up that child aspect of your inner community who most dominates your experience of life.

1. And you, little one, what is your name?
2. How old are you?
3. And how do you experience your life? (Repeat)
4. How do you experience Mother/Mommy/Mom? (Repeat)
5. How do you experience Father/Daddy/Papa? (Repeat)
6. What are you most afraid of? (Repeat)
7. What do you do when you are afraid? (Repeat)
8. When do you feel most helpless? (Repeat)
9. What do you do when you feel helpless? (Repeat)
10. What upsets you the most? (Repeat)
11. What do you do when you are upset? (Repeat)
12. What do you do to get attention? (Repeat)
13. What do you do when you can't get attention? (Repeat)
14. What do you do to get love? (Repeat)
15. What do you do when you can't get love? (Repeat)
16. What else would you like us to know about yourself? (Repeat)

Then center in your heart once again and let this aspect go. Just take a deep breath and allow this child aspect to recede into the background of your inner community. And then, from that centered place, call in a mature aspect

189

of your inner community, an aspect that has an overview of your totality and is able to recognize and label patterns. From the viewpoint of this mature aspect, how would you label or identify the aspect you just looked at? Was that an abandoned child speaking? A rejected child? How would you label it so you can recognize it in the future? And describe in a few sentences what major strategies this child aspect of your consciousness employs to get along in life.

If that child does not have a name different from the one you use in your adult life, you may wish to name it now. What do you want to call that little one?

Then take a deep breath and begin preparing to come back into an ordinary state of consciousness. Just let this all go and return to your outer awareness. When you are ready, open your eyes.

The Adolescent

The next part of the aspect process series will give you the opportunity to identify and become acquainted with the different adolescent aspects within your psyche. The first parts of the process, the set-up and the relaxation processes, are the same as for the Child Aspect Process. If you have not already read the set-up for that process above, please do so before beginning this one. Again, repeat the questions as indicated until no further responses are forthcoming. We present the relaxation process again here so you do not need to change pages and interrupt the exercise once you have begun.

Here it is:

With your eyes closed, imagine yourself in a room where you can feel very comfortable, very secure, and very relaxed. Take a look around the room and make sure everything is exactly the way you would like it to be. Have a place in the room to lie down. And then feel yourself lying down there and relaxing, becoming more and more comfortable.

Use your breath to allow your body to become more and more comfortable. Let go of any tension or tightness as you inhale, and release it as you exhale.

Visualize your feet, and visualize a golden liquid flowing into them through your toes. Know that everywhere this golden liquid passes, it is going to leave behind it soothing comfort, healing energy, and waves of relaxation.

Visualize the golden liquid flowing through your toes. Feel it moving soothingly and relaxingly through the muscles of your feet, up through your ankles and into your calves. Feel the golden liquid moving gently and relaxingly up through your knees and into your thighs. Consciously relax the long muscles of your thighs as the golden liquid fills your legs completely with waves of comfort and relaxation.

Then allow the golden liquid to move gently through your hips and pelvic area into your lower abdomen. Feel the golden liquid moving soothingly and relaxingly around and through the muscles and organs as it flows gently up your torso.

191

Allow the golden liquid to move through your solar plexus into your chest. Take a deep breath and, as you exhale, relax the muscles that surround your chest. Visualize the golden liquid flowing gently through the heart muscle, soothing and steadying your heartbeat.

Then allow the golden liquid to move up to your shoulders and begin flowing gently down into your upper arms. Allow the golden liquid to move gently down your arms, through your elbows, and down into your forearms.

Take a breath and relax. Feel the waves of comfort and relaxation moving soothingly down through your wrists, into your hands, and into your fingers. Then see the golden liquid moving gently up your neck and into your head, filling your head with waves of comfort and relaxation.

Now your body is completely filled with the soothing, relaxing, golden liquid.

Then mentally check out your body and notice if you feel any pockets of tension or tightness remaining anywhere. If you do, use your breath and visualize those tensions being dissolved into the golden liquid.

Know that this golden liquid will keep your body safe and protected, so you and you only can return to your body any time you choose. Then silently ask your own expanded consciousness to join in this process, requesting that it reveal to you the adolescent aspect of your totality who most dominates your experience of life.

[Pause. Then continue reading:]

Take a breath and center in your heart.

Call up that adolescent aspect of your inner community who most dominates your experience of life.

1. And you, what is your name?
2. And how old are you?
3. How do you experience your life? (Repeat)
4. How do you experience Mother/Mom? (Repeat)
5. How do you experience Father/Dad? (Repeat)
6. What angers you the most? (Repeat)
7. What do you do when you are angry? (Repeat)
8. When do you feel most helpless? (Repeat)
9. What do you do when you feel helpless? (Repeat)

10. When do you feel most misunderstood? (Repeat)
11. What do you do when you feel most misunderstood? (Repeat)
12. What embarrasses you the most? (Repeat)
13. What do you do when you are embarrassed? (Repeat)
14. What is most painful for you? (Repeat)
15. With regard to sex, what are you most afraid of? (Repeat)
16. What do you do when you are most afraid with regard to sex? (Repeat)
17. What do you do to get love? (Repeat)
18. What do you do when you can't get love? (Repeat)
19. What would you like the world to know? (Repeat)
20. What else do you want to use this opportunity to communicate? (Repeat)

Then center in your heart once again and let this aspect go. Just take a deep breath and allow this adolescent aspect to recede into the background of your inner community. And then, from that centered place, call in a mature aspect of your inner community, an aspect that has an overview of your totality and is able to recognize and label patterns. From the viewpoint of this mature aspect, how would you label or identify the aspect who was just speaking? Was it an insecure adolescent? A rebellious adolescent? A terrified adolescent? How would you label it so you can recognize it in the future? And describe in a few sentences what major strategies this adolescent aspect of your consciousness employs to get along in life.

If that adolescent aspect does not have a name different from the one you use in your adult life, you may wish to name it now.

Then take a deep breath and begin preparing to come back into an ordinary state of consciousness. Just let this all go and return to your outer awareness. When you are ready, open your eyes.

The Young Adult

The next part of the aspect process series will give you the opportunity to bring to consciousness the young adult aspects of your psyche. The first parts of the process, the set-up and the relaxation processes, are the same as for the child and adolescent aspect processes. If you have not already read the set-up for either of those processes above, please do so before beginning this one. Again, repeat the questions where such is indicated until no further responses are forthcoming. As before, we present the relaxation process again here, so you do not need to change pages and interrupt the exercise once you have begun.

Here is the process:

With your eyes closed, imagine yourself in a room where you can feel very comfortable, very secure, and very relaxed. Take a look around the room and make sure everything is exactly the way you would like it to be. Have a place in the room to lie down. And then feel yourself lying down there and relaxing, becoming more and more comfortable.

Use your breath to allow your body to become more and more comfortable. Let go of any tension or tightness as you inhale, and release it as you exhale.

Visualize your feet, and visualize a golden liquid flowing into them through your toes. Know that everywhere this golden liquid passes, it is going to leave behind it soothing comfort, healing energy, and waves of relaxation.

Visualize the golden liquid flowing through your toes. Feel it moving soothingly and relaxingly through the muscles of your feet, up through your ankles and into your calves. Feel the golden liquid moving gently and relaxingly up through your knees and into your thighs. Consciously relax the long muscles of your thighs as the golden liquid fills your legs completely with waves of comfort and relaxation.

Then allow the golden liquid to move gently through your hips and pelvic area into your lower abdomen. Feel the golden liquid moving soothingly and relaxingly around and through the muscles and organs as it flows gently up your torso.

Allow the golden liquid to move through your solar plexus into your chest. Take a deep breath and, as you exhale, relax the muscles that surround your chest. Visualize the golden liquid flowing gently through the heart muscle, soothing and steadying your heartbeat.

Then allow the golden liquid to move up to your shoulders and begin flowing gently down into your upper arms. Allow the golden liquid to move gently down your arms, through your elbows, and down into your forearms.

Take a breath and relax. Feel the waves of comfort and relaxation moving soothingly down through your wrists, into your hands, and into your fingers. Then see the golden liquid moving gently up your neck and into your head, filling your head with waves of comfort and relaxation.

Now your body is completely filled with the soothing, relaxing, golden liquid.

Then mentally check out your body and notice if you feel any pockets of tension or tightness remaining anywhere. If you do, use your breath and visualize those tensions being dissolved into the golden liquid.

Know that this golden liquid will keep your body safe and protected, so you and you only can return to your body any time you choose. Then silently ask your own expanded consciousness to join in this process, requesting that it reveal to you the young adult aspect of your totality who most dominates your experience of life.

[Pause. Then continue reading:]

Take a breath and center in your heart.

Call up that young adult aspect of your inner community who most dominates your experience of life.

1. What is your name?
2. How old are you?
3. How do you experience your life? (Repeat)
4. How is it for you to be in the world? (Repeat)
5. How do you experience Mother? (Repeat)
6. How do you experience Father? (Repeat)
7. With regard to your life, what do you hope to accomplish? (Repeat)
8. What do you find most difficult to accept about yourself? (Repeat)
9. How do you experience women? (Repeat)

10. With regard to women, what is most difficult for you to accept? (Repeat)
11. How do you experience men? (Repeat)
12. With regard to men, what is most difficult for you to accept? (Repeat)
13. How do you experience your sexuality? (Repeat)
14. With regard to your sexuality, what is most difficult for you to accept? (Repeat)
15. What are you most afraid of? (Repeat)
16. What do you do when you are afraid? (Repeat)
17. What upsets you the most? (Repeat)
18. What do you do when you are upset? (Repeat)
19. What do you do to get love? (Repeat)
20. What do you do when you can't get love? (Repeat)
21. What else do you want us to know about yourself? (Repeat)

Then center in your heart once again and let this aspect go. Just take a deep breath and allow this young adult aspect to recede into the background of your inner community. And then, from that centered place, call in a mature aspect of your inner community, an aspect that has an overview of your totality and is able to recognize and label patterns. From the viewpoint of this mature aspect, how would you label or identify the aspect who was just speaking? How would you label it so you can recognize it in the future? And describe in a few sentences what major strategies this young adult aspect of your consciousness employs to get along in life.

If that young adult does not have a name different from the one you use in your adult life, you may wish to name it now.

Then take a deep breath and begin preparing to come back into an ordinary state of consciousness. Just let this all go and return to your outer awareness. When you are ready, open your eyes.

You may apply this aspect process in many different ways. It is an excellent tool with which to explore your own multiplicity. From heart centeredness, you can—with confidence—explore many more dimensions of Being than we suggest here. We have mentioned these three stages—the child, the adolescent, and the young adult—since awareness of these aspects is crucial if you want to access the mature aspects of Being.

We recommend that you not consciously attempt to explore the transpersonal ranges of consciousness with this process until you are able to recognize the first three stages of development and how they are represented within your inner community. This is to assure that the younger ranges of the psyche do not attempt to claim the power of the transpersonal ranges for their own purposes. As you become more aware of these young aspects and how they tend to dominate your experience of life, and as you gain some ability to recognize them when they surface, you are more likely to be ready to enter other dimensions of Being. The realms of the transpersonal are no place for the children in us. Those children do not have the resources to handle the forces of the transpersonal ranges. Therefore, becoming conscious of our inner children and managing them is necessary when we begin to move into areas of experience that require the resources of our more mature aspects.

Communication

The communication exercise that follows is intended to support you and your partner in communicating in a way that is satisfying and which supports not only the intimacy between you but also your own personal awakening. First, there are a few things we'd like to say before getting to the actual exercise. Because communication is so crucial (and can be so frustrating), we find that having a few ground rules is useful for those times when communicating is difficult, or simply as a discipline to keep the lines of communication open between you.

A communication session can be used to say things you haven't said and/or to clean up things you have said or done that may get in the way of your relationship. It is a time to let go of thoughts that have nothing to do with the relationship but that are bothering you; to share frustrations or irritations that do have to do with the relationship; or simply as a time to make yourself vulnerable to your partner by sharing things you have noticed about yourself. All of this is much easier if you know you can count on being heard instead of reacted to. The session can take only a few seconds or can be quite lengthy. In either case, recognizing it specifically as a communication session is useful. Then both of you can give it your full attention and play by the rules.

If you can offer each other a safe opportunity to express yourself and to be heard, the love between you will blossom. Communicating in this way will also give both of you a chance to separate thoughts from reality. The realization that your thoughts about the world and other people, yourself included, do not necessarily reflect what is true can come as quite a shock.

Remember that sometimes you get caught in thoughts and they just whirl around in your head, consuming energy without serving any constructive purpose. When you talk about them, you release that energy so it can be applied more usefully. Being able to let thoughts go is a relief. Just being able to be heard is wonderful. Often a lot of energy that could have gone (or was going) into an upset simply will drop away through the experience of your having been heard.

Here are some tips:

First of all, *listening* is not *agreeing*. You can hear your partner without agreeing with what he or she is saying. You can "get" your partner's reality without having to have the same reality yourself. That is, in fact, the opportunity which is available in a communication session. You also have the chance to know your partner's reality—or at least the reality of one of his or her aspects—remembering that he or she has other aspects which may have a totally different experience of reality than the one currently being expressed.

Second, remember the process of projection. So, if your partner is expressing an upset with you, you can relax and listen, knowing that, in addition to whatever you may be responsible for, your partner is projecting his or her own unconscious material onto the screen you are graciously providing. That is not to say you are not involved. Your partner's issue is often a disguised version of your own issue as well. However, we all do project onto each other. Knowing that what upsets your partner may be something he or she has not taken responsibility for can make receiving your partner's communication a bit easier.

We need to be honest with ourselves and vulnerable with our partner. Again, the ego will do anything—use anything—to protect itself. It will use the most enlightened techniques or awareness against a loved one if that will allow it to defend itself against the possibility of losing control or experiencing pain. So, now that we know about projection, we must be aware that when our partner wants us to hear that something we have done (or said or not done or not said) has been upsetting or hurtful, we need to avoid the temptation to defend ourselves by accusing our partner of projecting. This is one of life's many paradoxes. Yes, others are projecting and at the same time we cannot dismiss what they are saying just because we know they are projecting. We also need to look honestly at our own part in the upset and be willing to be vulnerable enough to assume appropriate responsibility for what happened. We can take the opportunity to use what our partner is saying to become more aware of some of our own dynamics. We can find the courage to be honest and acknowledge that, yes, perhaps one of our child aspects did really want to hurt our partner or one of our destructive aspects did claim the microphone for a few moments in the spotlight. At the same time, other aspects of our inner community may regret what we said or did when those younger or destructive aspects were in charge.

For most of us, when we have something to say that we anticipate is going to be difficult and uncomfortable, either for ourselves or for the person we are talking to, we are ready for trouble. Even before we begin talking, we take on a defensive stance both physically and mentally. If we react to this defensive posture (which is usually based on fear) in the person speaking to us, we never get very far in hearing what is really being communicated. Again, knowing that what our partner is saying always discloses something about him or her in addition to whatever he or she may be saying about us is helpful, as it allows us to move beyond the style of presentation and provide that person with a space in which communication can occur.

Here is another (perhaps familiar) reminder. If you begin your sentences with "I" instead of "you," your listener is much less likely to become reactivated. This is basic. Saying, "I feel hurt that you forgot my birthday" is one thing. However, your listener is likely to react differently if you say, "You are so selfish, you never think about anyone but yourself. You can't even remember my birthday." Of course, "I" sentences are less popular with most of us, as they require vulnerability and responsibility. However, in the long run, the results are worth the momentary discomfort.

Sometimes, one of us—Gawain or Rhea—is so upset we just have to let it rip. That is to say, we do not want to be aware, or even rational, and we certainly don't want to use "I" sentences. These are the times when we just need to blow off steam. In those moments (if we are enough in touch with our center) we may say, "Look, I have something to say and I don't want to be responsible. I just want to dump!" If you want a dump session, or a finger-pointing session, as we like to call it, your partner must agree to it first, as it can be very hard for the listening partner to stay centered during a "dump." Such a session will only work if both partners are ready for it. The one receiving the dump really has to stay centered and breathe, so the energy moves through and doesn't get stuck somewhere inside.

Sometimes really pointing the finger, or dumping, is the easiest way to hear yourself so you can begin to see what you are projecting. Dumps are for emergency use only, however. We suggest that you practice the discipline and vulnerability of communicating responsibly whenever possible.

The first few times you do the process, we suggest that in order to have a successful communication session, you give yourself an hour or more without interruption. (Later, when you are more accustomed to communicating like this, you will need less and less of a formal set-up and you can just go at it whenever a session is needed.) Make sure the phone is off the hook or the answering machine is switched on. If you have children, arrange things so they won't disturb you. And, obviously, do whatever else is required for you to have an uninterrupted time together.

The exercise itself is simple. You just take turns saying everything you haven't said to each other. Sit opposite your partner. Decide who will talk first and who will listen first. Then close your eyes, hold hands, and center in the heart. The one who will be receiving the communication then indicates to the speaker when he or she is ready to hear what the other has to say. Let go of the hands, open your eyes, and make eye contact. Then the speaker begins and continues until he or she has said everything he or she has to say. When the speaker is finished both of you again close your eyes, hold hands, and center in the heart.

Now the one who was speaking indicates when he or she is ready to listen and you again let go of the hands, open your eyes, and make eye contact—then the second partner speaks until finished. Maintaining eye contact throughout the speaking is important. Equally important is to begin your sentences with "I" as much as possible. After you have had a few communication sessions, most of the "old stuff" will have come up and later you may need only a few minutes to clear your communication as you move through your life together.

You continue this process until each of you has said everything there is to say. You might each have to take two or three turns, since things often come up while you are listening. Remember that you need to be committed to completing the session in both directions. "Complete" means you are both satisfied—that you have said everything you have to say and you experienced being heard (not necessarily agreed with, but heard). If your partner is not complete, you are not complete.

In our Relationship Training, part of the initial homework is to have a communication session at the end of each evening to clear up anything that surfaced during the day. This homework is intended to establish a habit of open communication, which is something very few of us learned as we were growing up. The couples in the training report that they are surprised at how many upsets or potential upsets vanish as a result of just doing this simple exercise. That is also our experience in our relationship.

Meditation

Developing the spiritual side of yourself through your relationship may not have been part of your initial purpose in being together. However, since you are reading this book, we can assume you are now interested in the spiritual aspects of your relationship, whether or not you were conscious of them before.

Normally in relationship, couples connect with each other through the medium of the mind—that is, through the ability to relate to each other by sharing thoughts, memories, a sense of humor, expectations, hopes, fears, etc.—and through the body, emotions, and sexuality. Many people are satisfied with keeping the expression of their relationship on those levels. However our spiritual nature can also be consciously nurtured in relationship. We can see, experience, connect, and communicate in ways that go beyond the concerns of daily life, tapping into transpersonal levels with our partner—and that is truly divine.

Through meditation, we can glimpse the transcendent nature of ourselves, our partner, and the world. To experience this in relationship is a blessing and an addition to the experience of the ranges of our Beingness. To experience our partner as a divine manifestation, as Spirit in form, creates a deep communion and inner peace.

Profound forces are always at play in any intimate relationship, forces that have little to do with the mundane levels where the relationship usually operates. Becoming *aware* of those forces and acknowledging them consciously within the framework of a relationship adds incredible richness to a relationship and to life. A new world opens that is beyond anything we have previously known, a world of living in the moment, of immediate experience, of a here-and-nowness that leaves all ideas and assumptions, all habits of thought and judgment about our partner and about ourselves, far behind.

Sharing the spiritual side of life in any relationship is supportive of the relationship. In a committed partnership, a certain wonder is added to the relationship when both partners are aligned in the awareness that life is a mystery play in which each of us shares a tiny part, as though we were a drop of dew in the morning sun, soon to vanish from physical existence. Again, even if it is not consciously manifested, a spiritual side is always present in a love relationship because all of us have a spiritual nature, whether we experience it or not. Some spiritual connection must exist, or you wouldn't be together. However, you may not be acknowledging this connection; you may not consciously be nurturing it. Meditation is one way to consciously engage the spiritual dimension of your relationship.

When you first catch a glimpse of this dimension of your life together, your relationship transforms. It sheds an outer skin. New possibilities in the quality of being together begin to unfold.

Since we deal with the spiritual side of life in the seminars we lead together, we get frequent glimpses of the spiritual dimension of human life and are often humbled by it. We realize, of course, that not many people are in our situation—involved together professionally in the spiritual arena. However, anyone can still share a life that is consciously centered on the transcendent nature of what it means to be human.

Meditating together can support the spiritual parts of you as individuals and the spiritual dimension of your relationship. Through meditation, you have the opportunity to gain distance from the movements of your mind. What do we mean by that? By now, you are no doubt well aware of the incessant claims of your thoughts, desires, ideas, attitudes, and judgments. The mind never stops its commentary. Most people live out their lives without ever having experienced distance from this "monkey mind" (so called because, like a monkey, it is all over the place). Most of us are pulled through life as if the vicissitudes of the mind actually have something to do with reality.

As you might remember from the section on projection, the mind projects its dynamics onto the screen of outer reality and then thinks that what it sees is real. The truth is that what it sees is a reflection of itself and not necessarily what is really out there. Much too easily do we give authority to the incessant chatter in our heads. It is a shock to recognize that, contrary to popular opinion, the mind is not the highest authority in the universe.

If we can get a break from this nonstop inner monologue, we find ourselves suddenly refreshed and looking at our life with a new perspective. This can happen through meditation. In our own relationship, potentially difficult situations often dissolved after we meditated together. After sitting together in meditation, we are often in touch with the essence of our Beinghood, and that has a big influence on what happens in our relationship. Meditation creates awareness, inner silence, a space for introspection, and a distance from what often seems to be so important to the outer mind. Meditation deflates the self-importance of the ego. (That, in itself, is a boon to any relationship!)

We recommend a daily discipline of meditating together (we sit together and meditate almost every morning for at least twenty minutes). If your schedule doesn't allow time for daily meditation, set aside some time on the weekend and reserve it for that purpose. Meditation is another kind of inner hygiene. Just like honest communication and self-expression, it is a very important part of anyone's psychic health and inner balance. Once you experience the difference meditating together can make, you may find that getting up twenty-five minutes earlier every day is worth the loss of sleep.

You may chose a quiet, sitting meditation or an active, dynamic kind of movement meditation. The active meditations we mention here are best done to music. You may wish to read the instructions first, then select appropriate music from your own music library. Or, you may wish to purchase the music that has been specially created for these meditations. If neither music resource is available to you, you can simply imagine suitable rhythms and do your best to create your own inner accompaniment.

Perhaps you will alternate between active and passive types of meditating. There is a wide variety of both types of meditation, and people have to find the type that works best for them. If you have never meditated, we suggest that you begin with an active type, since average, modern Westerners carry a lot of restless energy in their bodies, and an active meditation will help release that energy and prepare you for a sitting meditation.

Because our lifestyle has changed remarkably during the last few hundred years, traditional meditations that have been practiced through the centuries often must be modified to meet present reality. Twenty-five hundred years ago, for example, when the Buddha recommended a meditation that consisted of just sitting quietly and watching one's breath, the average human being was accustomed to much hard, physical labor as a part of normal daily life. The body responds differently to stillness when one has been using it vigorously for ten hours a day. Also, life was not as complex back then. The rhythm of a person's daily life was much slower-paced and more predictable.

Today, however, most of us live a more sedentary existence. Additionally, through the mass media, we are constantly aware of what is happening, not only in our local area but also in the world. We are exposed to complexities and forces that people were not consciously aware of even a century ago. This is a lot for the average person to carry. On the one hand, it makes meditation—the practice of quieting the mind—even more necessary. On the other hand, it makes meditation more difficult—for the same reason.

We have noticed in our seminars that most people find it very difficult to begin their experience of meditation in the traditional way. Sitting still, apparently doing nothing, for anything more than ten minutes is not easy for the average person. Perhaps you can relate to that. Initially, people seem to find it easier to experience the benefits of meditation through some kind of physically active practice.

Active meditations usually consist of several different phases. In the beginning, one can often release the body's energies through chaotic dancing or breathing or some other kind of bodywork. This gives one the opportunity to let go of all that restless energy, the energy most people in our culture seem to accumulate. After the chaotic, or release, phase of most active meditations, there is a quiet, sitting phase. Being still and tuning in to one's interior is much easier after one has fully participated in the chaotic portion of a meditation.

Some examples of these kinds of meditations are: the Five-Rhythm Meditation, created by Gabrielle Roth; the Dynamic and Kundalini meditations, created by Osho; the Body-Flow and Soma Meditations, created by Michael Barnett; and the Kali Meditation, which we have created. Any of these will provide a good beginning in the art of active meditation. As representative of this group of meditations, we will present the Five-Rhythm and the Kali meditations, which we often use in our seminars.

The Five-Rhythm Meditation

The Five-Rhythm meditation was created by Gabrielle Roth, a wonderful modern shaman who lives in New York City with her husband and collaborator, Robert. Gabrielle has noticed that all human movement falls into one or more of five basic rhythms. The first movement she recognizes is *round and flowing*. It is a continuous, undulating movement, and has a feminine feel to it. The second pattern of movement she distinguishes is *staccato*. It has a beginning, a middle, and an end. In feel, it is more masculine. The next pattern is *chaotic*. (Chaos being what some of us think naturally happens when the feminine and masculine meet!) The phase after the chaotic, Gabrielle calls *lyrical*. After old structures are released through chaos, the lyrical movement represents a new order, a settling down into new form after the destruction of the old. The next natural rhythm is *stillness*.

Gabrielle points out that this sequence of rhythms is present in the most basic of human activities, including making love and giving birth. We agree that moving through the five basic rhythms in this meditation touches something very elemental in one's humanness. (Gabrielle works with the five rhythms less as a meditation and more as an expression of art in motion. Her work is wonderfully inspiring and we highly recommend it. Gabrielle also has written a book, titled *Maps to Ecstasy*.)

The Five-Rhythm Meditation may be done to your own music or to your own imagined, inner accompaniment, though it can best be done to a wonderful piece of music called *Initiation*, which Gabrielle and Robert have created specifically for this meditation. The audio cassette tape and the CD are available in most spiritual bookstores. The following instructions are intended for readers who have the tape or the CD, but can be easily adapted, as necessary, for those who do not.

You begin the meditation standing evenly supported on both legs. The knees should be slightly bent and the shoulders and jaw relaxed. Then experience the energy of Earth, that which comes from below. Feel, experience, visualize that energy entering your body through the soles of your feet and gradually filling your whole body. Then begin allowing your body to move in the round and flowing way. The music will support your movement. Have the experience that the round and flowing aspect of the feminine awakens within you. Feel one movement merging and melting into the next in an uninterrupted flow. These movements might take you to the floor and/or across the room. Follow wherever the movement takes you. When the music ends, allow these round and flowing movements to subside and prepare to shift into staccato movement.

When the new music track begins, find the energy within you that is staccato—a sharp, fragmented energy that has a beginning, middle, and an end . . . beginning, middle, end. Over and over again. Find that aspect of the masculine that is staccato, that can penetrate, pierce, and intrude. When the music ends, allow these movements to subside and prepare for chaos.

When the chaos track begins, allow your body the freedom to move beyond the conditioned responses that usually determine how you move. Allow your body to express whatever is chaotic within you. If you can't find any chaos inside at first, just make it up—act it. You will very likely find that your body will take the cue and bring the chaotic material up for you to experience. Give yourself permission to just surrender to the movement of your body. This is a great opportunity to let go of control in a safe way.

After the chaotic phase ends and the lyrical phase begins (you will hear it clearly in the music), there are no specific instructions except just to let the body decide what it wants to do. Anything is permitted except sitting or lying down. Feel into the body; listen to what is happening inside. If the chaotic phase has been done totally, you will feel a new balance of the forces within you coming forward during the lyrical part of the meditation. Follow the body and allow it to express this after-chaos state.

The last part of the meditation is silence. Again the shift is indicated by a shift in the music. For this last phase, either sit or stand, with eyes closed and your focus turned inward. As a silent witness, watch whatever is going on inside. Just observe whatever is moving through you, without becoming involved.

The Kali Meditation

Kali is the consort of Shiva, the Hindu god of destruction. We developed the Kali Meditation because we saw a need to create a structure in which the forces of destruction could be consciously honored. For Hindus, God has three faces: Brahma, the creator or *G*enerator; Vishnu, the maintainer or *O*perator; and Shiva, the *D*estroyer. In English that works out nicely— G O D!

In our society, with its essentially Christian background, we do not have much tolerance for the destructive energies. They are usually considered among the darker forces, and are either excluded or demonized. We fail to recognize that although these forces are not consciously honored, they nevertheless seek acknowledgment by surfacing in many forms, such as urban strife, violence, and, however righteously it may be excused, war. The approaches offered by the Hindu religion and by Tibetan Buddhism seem much wiser than those presented by the Christianity-based religions, in that they acknowledge wrathful aspects of the godhead. The Christian religion relegates all the negative to Lucifer, who is not included in the perception of God, but rather is split off from God as an antagonist.

Since we—Rhea and Gawain—feel that the feminine force is actively surfacing in human affairs right now in order to bring balance and to create a new possibility for synthesis of the masculine and feminine energies, we acknowledge and honor the destructive aspect of the feminine in this meditation. We feel that the chaotic, destructive aspect of the feminine has been suppressed in our culture for too long. By honoring this energy consciously, by giving it a conscious space in your life through the ritual of meditation, you will not need to dramatize the destructive force unconsciously in your daily experience.

The following instructions are intended for those of you who have the music created by Gawain especially for this meditation. (For information about ordering either the audio tape or the CD, write to us at the address given on the copyright page of this book.) However, as with the Five-Rhythm Meditation, you can, after reading these instructions, compile suitable music from your own library or create an appropriate inner accompaniment.

As with other active meditations, the more totally you do this, the more you will get out of it. Make sure you will not be disturbed for at least an hour. You will want to do the meditation in a place where you have plenty of room to move and where you can play the music as loud as possible. We suggest that you wear a blindfold to support you in staying in touch with your internal process.

The meditation has four phases: Part One is a ten-minute breathing section, beginning with a 4/4 breathing rhythm. Inhale deeply on the first beat. Then exhale on the next three beats until you have the feeling that there is no more air in your lungs. Breathe in this rhythm, using your whole body, until the music starts to become more and more complex. Then slowly change your breathing rhythm from the 4/4 to a chaotic rhythm, emphasizing the exhalation. The purpose of this initial phase is to create an opening in your emotional body to allow the destructive force to come to the surface.

Part Two is the expression of the Kali, or destructive, force. Use the driving rhythm of the music to support you in expressing that energy through movement and voice. When expressing the power of the voice, use gibberish—syllables and sounds that don't belong to any language, that don't make sense to the mind. In this way you will not hook your mind, and staying connected to the dynamic experience of expressing the force associated with Kali will be much easier.

Part Three of the meditation is simply standing. Allow all movements and sounds to slowly come to rest, until there is a sense of silence in the body. Silently look inside as consciously and attentively as possible.

Part Four is either sitting quietly or lying down. As completely as you can, let go of everything that has happened and allow yourself to come to rest. Just be there. A gong will sound announcing the end of the meditation.

This meditation, if done when you feel it is needed, will give you a conscious way of expressing the destructive energies in yourself and in your body. Too often when these destructive forces begin to surface, we unconsciously dramatize them with those around us. Thus, having a space available to let go of destructive energy consciously and safely when it begins to surface is a great relief. Being able to honor the destructive force without getting that energy all over your partner is wonderful. Try it!

Energy Meditations

There are many different types of quiet, or passive meditations available. For example, there is Za-Zen, the Japanese form of meditation in which one sits quietly, with eyes open, softly focused on one spot. In this style of meditation, focusing on a (seemingly) solid external object or scene is experientially contrasted to the fluctuations of the mind and feelings. Then there is the Indian way of sitting quietly with the eyes closed and focusing on the breath going in and out. Again, the intention is to allow thoughts and feelings to float by without becoming attached to them—to observe the "monkey mind" and begin to open to other parts of oneself than the mind. Of the quiet, sitting meditations, we recommend the heart centering technique described at the beginning of this section. Beginning the day by re-initiating yourself into the attributes of the Heart Center is very supportive of your spiritual journey. However, simply sitting quietly with a comfortably straight back and focusing on your breath is also a powerful meditative tool for self-discovery.

Some other powerful meditations involve what we call "energy work." The following describes some of the principles behind that work and gives exercises and meditations that people in our seminars have found particularly useful.

Talking about an individual's perception of the energy nature of reality is not easy, since the experience is highly subjective and different people will be conscious of it in different ways. We can point to what is possible but cannot tell you exactly what you will experience. All attempts to bring energy meditation into a precise conceptual framework are necessarily limited. It is one of those things in life that cannot be fully and accurately explained in words. Like sex, only the experience of it will give you a glimpse into this aspect of the mystery of your Being. Nevertheless, we will attempt to describe the nature of energy work as we have experienced it and as some people in our seminars have reported experiencing it. Later we will describe three exercises that can give you an opportunity to experience energy work for yourself.

The energy aspect of consciousness can connect you to a dimension of Being that is very different from the dimensions you are accustomed to experiencing. From this aspect of consciousness, you can see and/or feel that you are surrounded by an invisible energy field, often called the aura. It surrounds the body like a luminous egg, radiating energy all the time, in all directions, while simultaneously also receiving energy from everything around it. The aura is made up of fine tentacles, or energy lines, that shine forth from the body. These tentacles, or energy lines, interact with everything they meet. You might visualize these lines as a spider's web. Just as when you touch a strand of a spider's web the whole web moves, so does the movement of one energy line affect and influence the rest of the energy field. When the energy field of your body comes into contact with other energy fields (not only those of other people but also those of animals or plants), you can experience many different sensations and feelings.

When you experience life from such a state of awareness, you have the feeling that you are connected to everything surrounding you and that everything surrounding you is connected to you. When your partner turns his/her head, you feel it physically. When a cat passes you a few feet away, you feel her energy as if she had actually physically touched you. Many other variations of these kinds of experiences can occur when you are consciously aware of the energy field that surrounds you. People in our seminars report an increased sensitivity of the senses. As in the heart centering meditation, the speed with which you are experiencing the world seems to slow down.

In addition to what is common for most people, various distinct and individual experiences of the energy realm are also reported. Some people see the energy lines as radiant, shining threads, while others feel them physically in their bodies and/or through their hands, as if the energy lines were fine threads or thick ropes. They feel the energy lines in, through, and with their hands. Hands that are connected to those lines can stay suspended upright in the air for more than forty-five minutes without effort. If you tried to hold up your hand for that long while you were in an ordinary state of consciousness, you, like most people, would give up after five minutes. Try it.

Others don't experience any of those phenomena but have an increased sense of what one might call intuition. In this state of awareness, which we call the energy space, they suddenly are able to notice clearly some of the patterns that are determining their lives, or they get insight into how to solve a problem they have been having. Other people don't seem to have any remarkable experience to report. They just feel very relaxed and good. The state of being that is generated by energy work seems to remove them from the concerns of daily life and bring them into contact with some essential part of their nature.

In addition to the rather mystical experience associated with energy work, we have also found an application for energy work in daily life and in relationship. Once you find your way into this energy dimension, you start to discover how much it affects what seems to be outer reality. You then have the opportunity to discover that your emotions, thoughts, body sensations, attitudes, feelings, ideas, and all the images of the mind consist of energy structures. Our experience is that all of these human experiences— from thoughts to emotions, from the experience of pain to the experience of ecstasy—are animated by an energy or force that you can experience directly rather than through the manifestations the energy later acquires.

Here is an analogy. Imagine air being pumped through a pipe organ. The air is analogous to energy. The different pipes represent the different emotions, thoughts, and body sensations. And the organ itself is the whole body. In energy work, what essentially happens is that you connect with the air before it is pumped through the various pipes, and you experience it directly. Later, with practice, you can even determine through which pipe the energy is about to flow. So when the song that is about to be played is jealousy, you can directly experience, as an energy vibration, the energy that is going to become jealousy, or you can even choose to re-route it through another pipe—perhaps ecstasy or joy—and in this way play a new song on the same organ.

Let's look at an example. Say you are feeling jealousy because your partner seems attracted to someone else. If you stay with the experience on the level of the mind—thinking, worrying, and processing all the fears—you will tend to bring up your defenses against the feelings and the pain they contain. The chances are that you will create a corresponding drama in outer reality. You may scream at your partner or withdraw or somehow try to hurt your partner or try to make him or her feel guilty. If, on the other hand, you feel the energy that you normally associate with the experience called jealousy beginning to gather inside you and then experience it at an energy level, you can connect with yourself in a much more essential way. In other words, you go into that part of yourself where you can feel your reaction as a vibration of energy and experience that energy directly rather than waiting until it turns into thoughts or even emotions. On an energy level, your reaction might include a shaking of your body. Or sounds might come. Your body might contort on the floor, or perhaps you would just remain silent and experience bliss. All of these reactions are possible.

Fourteen years ago, during the time when I—Gawain—lived in New York, I had a wonderful new girlfriend with whom I was deeply in love. Just a week before, I had done a workshop with a man called Somendra, through whom I first became acquainted with energy work the way I describe it here. One evening as I returned home from work to the ashram where I lived, I saw my new girlfriend hugging and kissing a good friend of mine. All my systems went on red alert: *pain is coming, pain is coming, red light, red light.* Since they hadn't noticed me yet, I was ready to sneak out of sight, lest they finish their embrace, turn around, and see me being embarrassed and hurt. Suddenly I remembered the energy work I had experienced just a week earlier, in which the teacher told us that all these emotions could be experienced directly, at the energy level. Somehow I decided, through the beginning fog of my emotional shock, to stay conscious enough to give it a try. I sat down on a little wall in front of our ashram, closed my eyes, and connected with this energy aspect—an aspect with which, I had discovered a week previously, I can connect pretty easily. After some time, while my thoughts were screaming bloody murder and my stomach started to contract in an effort to deal with this thing called jealousy; while the mixture of shame, embarrassment, and anger moved my facial muscles every which way; I opened to my experience of the energy aspect. My body started to shake, my breathing pattern changed, I felt a swirling energy in my belly, and after a little while a deep laughter started to emerge from my belly. Eyes closed, I sat there on the wall and laughed and laughed. Later, that laughter turned into a profound, silent bliss.

Fifteen minutes later, when I opened my eyes, I saw the two people looking at me with worried expressions on their faces, obviously wondering what was going on with me. I just smiled and felt an overwhelming sense of love for both of them. Later I shared my experience with them verbally. My relationship with my girlfriend continued without my having to deal with any of the resentment or anger that her hugging and kissing my friend could have brought up had I not experienced it on this energy level. For me that was a great demonstration of the power of energy awareness.

Being aware and conscious of your energy body can allow you to experience yourself in a much more essential way than is possible through the mind. When you are living life in a relationship, this can be very helpful, since so much of the conflict in a relationship is a result of defensive strategies intended to avoid pain. If, instead of reacting to an outer event, we choose to experience the event on an inner energy level, we can have a direct experience of the event without any strategy in the realm of the mind, on a level where there is only vibration and the flow of energy.

Connecting with these levels is easier for some people than for others. We often do energy work in our seminars in which we induct participants into these levels, and there are always a few who don't seem to be able to experience the energy space. Whether the experience comes naturally to you or not, we highly recommend that you experiment with energy work and see where it takes you.

The first step in opening to this work is to do the exercise called "Into the Abyss," in which you look into each other's eyes without blinking. The next step is to learn to use your eyes to become sensitive to energy fields.

We are conditioned from early childhood in regard to how we use our eyes. Children often report seeing a figure in their room who is comforting them or talking to them, observing that their "friend" can walk through walls. Usually, when children wondrously tell their parents about such phenomena, they are told they are talking nonsense, or that what they see doesn't exist. Or the worried parents might even bring their youngster to a child psychologist, thinking something is wrong. Thus, as a result of parental pressure and young children's dependence on and desire to please their parents, children teach themselves not to notice certain aspects of reality. They literally teach their eyes not to see those things that don't fit into the consensus reality of the adults around them.

You can, however, retrain your eyes to perceive aspects of reality of which you have not been conscious. Generally, the more relaxed your eyes are when you look at something, the more you will be able to perceive the energies that are usually shut out by the filtering mechanism of the mind. In many cases, you can learn to see that energy by using your eyes in the way we described in the exercise called "Dragon Eyes."

The last step in our introduction to energy work in this book is a partner exercise, which will give you the opportunity to experience energy work with someone with whom you have an intimate relationship.

When you and your partner give yourselves the opportunity to explore such new vistas of experience, you also bond newly and another level of connectedness opens to you. Habit and monotony are deadly in relationship. Experiencing life on an energy level can open you to ranges of reality that will stimulate your aliveness and expand your experience of who you really are.

Into the Abyss

Here is one way to start the exploration into energy aspects of reality. First, sit opposite your partner. Sit fairly close to one another, either on chairs or on the floor, so your knees are almost touching, but not quite. Then hold hands and close your eyes. Center in the heart. When you feel ready, open your eyes. Whether one of you opens your eyes a little earlier than the other doesn't matter.

Let go of your partner's hands and look into his/her eyes, concentrating on the space between the eyes, above the nose. Relax your gaze and keep looking at this spot for twenty minutes—without (and this is not easy) blinking your eyes. Although there will be a strong temptation to blink, see if you can avoid doing so. You don't need to worry; this exercise will not hurt your eyes. (We have done it many times and our eyes are fine.) You might want to set an alarm clock so you don't have to look away to check the time. Then, after the twenty minutes are over, close your eyes again and hold hands with your partner. After a short time, come back into your everyday awareness and share with each other what went on for you.

This exercise is a remarkably easy way to begin opening to the experience of the nonsolidity of physical reality. When looking at a partner in this way, many people experience changes in their partner's face. Sometimes the partner vanishes and what is left is just the eyes, or just white light. Many other experiences are possible. Try it and see what happens for you!

"Into the Abyss" can also open you up to an incredible depth of perception about the mystery of life your partner represents. We usually think our knowledge of the world is reliable, and we are frequently shocked to realize suddenly that we don't have a clue about who and what is really around us. If you have read Carlos Castaneda's book *Journey to Ixlan*, you may remember a scene in which Carlos, pushed by his shaman teacher, Don Juan, experiences that he is alone in the world, surrounded only by images without substance, by illusion. He also realizes that what he assumed was a solidly founded experience of daily life was quite different when he shifted the way he perceived reality.

217

Dragon Eyes

The instructions for this exercise* are to be followed by both partners at the same time. Sit opposite your partner in such a way that your knees almost touch. Hold hands and close your eyes. Tune in to your partner's energy through his/her hands, as if your own hands were sensitive instruments that could experience and know your partner on many levels without the need of the thinking process. After a while, let go of your partner's hands, rest your hands palms-up on your knees, and open your eyes. Look at the space on your partner's face just below the nose and above the upper lip. Rest your eyes on this spot and look at it with a sharply focused gaze—as if your gaze were an arrow zooming in on it. Hold that focused gaze for about half a minute. Then slowly start to relax your eyes, keeping them centered on that spot, but relaxing them more and more.

After a while your eyes will begin to see more and more of your partner's face, your partner's body, and the space around your partner. When your eyes are completely relaxed and open to your partner, you will even see parts of yourself. Keep your eyes on the same place below the nose and hold this look with a wide-open, relaxed gaze.

The following eye movements are then done in synchronization with your partner. After about two or three minutes, start moving the center of this gaze down your partner's body, until the focus of your gaze rests on his/her genital area. Then move your gaze up your partner's body until it rests two to three inches above his/her head. Then once more, slowly and consciously, direct your gaze all the way down to the genital area. While you are doing this, keep your eyes as relaxed and open as you can, without contracting them again into a sharp focus.

The second time you move your gaze slowly up your partner's body, let your eyes choose where to rest, as if they are being irresistibly drawn to one spot on your partner's body or close to the body, in its aura. Do not let your mind come in with its preferences or biases. Just let your eyes be drawn to

---

* Based on a process developed by Michael Barnett. Michael, who teaches energy work in Europe, lives with a group of students in central France.

where they want to go and hold your gaze on that spot. Remember to relax your eyes and not to contract your focus.

As you look at the spot your eyes have selected, open yourself even further through your eyes by relaxing them more and more. Then gently take one of your fingers and lift it up. Just take the hand and finger that want to move from the knee in response to this instruction. Which finger responds does not matter. Lift the finger and hand up slowly and consciously in the space in front of you. As you do this, your finger is still close to you and your eyes are still focused on your partner. Feel how the finger becomes energized by the energy around and within you.

As you did before with the gazing, do this movement synchronously with your partner. Then each of you slowly points your finger in the direction of the spot you are observing, but does not touch the spot. After some time, when doing so feels right, slowly move your finger toward the spot your eyes are looking at. Then finally touch the spot and, as you do, close your eyes. Allow to happen whatever wants to happen as a result of this contact, without letting your mind interfere. You may feel movement, emotion, stillness—just let whatever is authentically there for you happen. Stay in your feelings and stay with your body sensations.

Then, after a while, as you sense that the experience is coming to completion, slowly withdraw your finger and gently bring it back to any place on your own body it feels drawn to. At that point, allow to happen what wants to happen without any interference from your thinking process. Then when you feel the exercise is complete, return your hand to your knee and, when you are ready, open your eyes, returning to your outer levels of awareness.

On the Razor's Edge
(Walking on Energy Lines)

This next exercise[*] builds on the two exercises just described. As we have indicated, people can relate to each other in many different ways, depending on their state of mind. You can relate to others on the mental, intellectual, social, and emotional planes by sharing thoughts and ideas, by telling them of your love, anger, annoyance, appreciation, and so on. You can relate to them silently through eye contact. We all have, at one time or another, used our eyes to communicate attraction ("You see a face across a crowded room . . . ") or anger (If looks could kill!). You can relate to others through touch. You can also relate to another Being on an energy level.

Walking "on energy lines" with your partner has the power to return you immediately to a deep part within yourself and allows you to experience yourself as an energy Being, beyond the mechanics of the mind.

In this exercise we will work with the eyes, much as we did in the previous exercise. You and your partner begin by standing opposite each other, about thirty feet apart, with a clear space between you. Being barefoot and dressed in comfortable clothes is best. Each of you stands with your body relaxed, paying particular attention to your knees, shoulders, and jaw, as those are the places most of us carry tension. Have your arms hanging at your sides, with the palms facing forward.

Look at a place on the floor midway between yourself and your partner. Sharply focus your gaze on that spot for about half a minute. Then, while still looking at that spot, begin to relax your eyes.

As in the earlier exercise, allow your eyes to relax so you gradually see most of the space around you, including parts of your own body. Allow your eyes to stay relaxed for some time. (Suggesting a specific length of time is difficult, since time expands when you are in this state of awareness and thinking about minutes or seconds is distracting. You simply have to sense what feels right for you—which is not a bad exercise in itself!)

---

[*] Based on a process developed by Michael Barnett.

After a while, slowly and consciously bring your relaxed gaze across the remaining space between you to the spot where your partner's feet meet the ground. Then contract your focus again until you see only your partner's feet and the floor where he/she is standing. After some time, begin to relax your eyes, as if they were flowers opening in the morning sun. Then, as you did in the last exercise, slowly scan your partner with this relaxed gaze, moving your eyes slowly and consciously all the way up and down your partner's body. As with the previous exercise, the second time you move your gaze up the body, allow your eyes to rest on a spot they want to look at. Just let your eyes stop on the spot they feel drawn to. Then relax your eyes even further.

As you stand there looking at this spot, know that whatever you look at also looks at you. Know that the spot you are looking at might have something for you, something your own energy body needs. Your eyes have not chosen this spot at random. Your intuition, working through your eyes, chose that spot. So begin opening to the place you are looking at, as if an energy line were connecting you to it. Experience this energy line getting stronger the more you look at it in this relaxed and open way.

After some time, when doing so feels right, you and your partner begin walking toward each other very slowly, feeling into the energy that now connects you. As you will discover, this is not a "regular" walk. Be open to the reactions of your body. Your body may shake or twist. You may feel a desire to make strange sounds. Allow your body to respond in any way it wants to as you slowly walk toward your partner. When your bodies meet, be open to the contact. Allow whatever wants to happen to happen— regardless of what it may be. Allow yourself to set your thinking mind aside, and stay in your experience.

We all have certain ways of being with people (even those closest to us) that are dominated by our patterns, our conditioning, and our attitudes. An energy exercise such as this allows us to connect with people on a soul level, on an essential energy level, where the nourishment of human contact is amplified to a greater level than it is on the outer levels of social reality.

What do you really want from a partner? Our experience is that we all want real contact, a deep connection with the essence of the other. Usually that does not come about as a result of our daily interactions. We are often sidetracked by the maze of the mind, or simply too preoccupied with the logistics of life, and we don't experience the deep connection we are all longing for. Through this exercise, you can bypass the maze and directly touch the deep central core of your own essence and the essence of your partner. When there is disharmony in your relationship and you have the presence of mind to stay centered despite the emotional turmoil, opening to this exercise can reconnect you to what is essential between you and your partner.